THE MODERNIZATION OF POVERTY

SOCIAL, ECONOMIC AND POLITICAL STUDIES OF THE MIDDLE EAST

ÉTUDES SOCIALES, ÉCONOMIQUES ET POLITIQUES DU MOYEN ORIENT

VOLUME XIII

GALAL A. AMIN

THE MODERNIZATION OF POVERTY

LEIDEN
E. J. BRILL
1974

THE MODERNIZATION OF POVERTY

A STUDY IN THE POLITICAL ECONOMY OF GROWTH IN NINE ARAB COUNTRIES
1945 - 1970

BY

GALAL A. AMIN

With 35 Tables

LEIDEN
E. J. BRILL
1974

Le but de la collection est de faciliter la communication entre le grand public international et les spécialistes des sciences sociales étudiant le Moyen-Orient, et notamment ceux qui y résident. Les ouvrages sélectionnés porteront sur les phénomènes et problèmes contemporains: sociaux, culturels, économiques et administratifs. Leurs principales orientations relèveront de la théorie générale, de problématiques plus précises, et de la politologie: aménagement des institutions et administration des affaires publiques.

The series is designed to serve as a link between the international reading public and social scientists studying the contemporary Middle East, notably those living in the area. Works to be included will be characterized by their relevance to actual phenomena and problems: whether social, cultural, economic, political or administrative. They will be theory-oriented, problem-oriented or policy-oriented.

ISBN 90 04 03969 4

PRINTED IN THE NETHERLANDS

"Economic theory will remain a steel construction built on foundations of sand until our understanding of non-economic factors is brought to the same level of generality and sophistication as the study of strictly economic matters, so that economic and sociological theory form a continuum. That we are still very far from this goal is not only the fault of isolationist economists but also the consequence of the sterility of the contemporary sociological theory which... is being turned into a meaningless jargon by the most influential of its present exponents."

S. Andreski, *The African Predicament*, 1969.

To my children

Danya, Tamer and Ahmad

in the hope that their future
may be a little more prosperous
and less modern

CONTENTS

LIST OF TABLES

PREFACE

The aim of this essay is not to give a complete account of Arab economic performance since the War, but rather to account for what went wrong. The more favourable aspects may not, therefore, have received sufficient attention, but it is still hoped that the truth has not suffered as a result. Although the reader is warned of this, it is hoped that some will welcome it.

Dissatisfaction with the Arab economic scene is not the feeling of a mere minority. Although this dissatisfaction provokes ceaseless conversation among Arab as well as foreign economists, not excluding U.N. experts, what they write on the Arab world in their more guarded moments often gives exactly the opposite impression. The present essay is not likely therefore to be more than a drop in an ocean of flattering, over-"diplomatic" or over-optimistic literature.

But because there is no hope of understanding the deficiencies of Arab economic performance or the real obstacles to future development without due attention being paid to political factors, this essay contains almost as much politics as economics. And it is largely because of this that, at several points, the approach may seem somewhat personal and even passionate. No apology will be made, however, either for the politics or for the passion. If personal judgements seem almost to have disappeared from economic writing and if the expression of the writer's passion, however mild, has become taboo, it is largely because political and social issues are excluded. But it is precisely this exclusion which seems to result in a greater misrepresentation of the truth about the Arab world than any liberty which the writer may take in expressing his personal judgements. It is indeed probable that readers of the future will be genuinely surprised to find that, as late as 1971, a Swedish economist found it necessary to stress to his fellow social scientists that "there are no economic problems, there are simply problems and they are complex",[1] and that a British economist was recently so angered by the fact that social scientists often regard certain social phenomena as unimportant simply because they are not measurable.[2]

---

[1] Myrdal, G.: *The Challenge of World Poverty*, Pelican, 1971, p. 30.

[2] "Such is our perverse faith in figures that what cannot be quantified is all too often left out of the calculus altogether. There is apparently a strong prejudice among researh workers against admitting that the unmeasurable effects are likely to

One of the main themes of this study is that, in spite of their different beginnings a quarter of a century ago, as time went by, Arab countries came to display strong similarities. Foreign observers and social scientists, however, for reasons that are not far to seek, show a general preference for emphasizing their differences. Because of an artificial dichotomy between economics and politics the different leanings of Arab governments with regard to foreign policy seem to have precedence over the much more important fact, from the point of view of development, that all of them are heavily dependent on the good will of some foreign power. For the same reason the abundance of foreign exchange in some countries is repeatedly contrasted to its scarcity in others to the neglect of the more important common fact that in all of them a considerable part of this foreign exchange is wasted. Because of an exaggerated concern with average incomes, to the neglect of income distribution, the relative affluence of Lebanon, Libya, and of course Kuwait is unduly emphasized. The fact is, however, that income inequalities in these, as well as in the poorer Arab countries, make for much less significant differences between them with regard both to the level of income of lower-income groups and to the way of life of the minorities at the top. Again, as a result of an exaggerated regard for legal forms too much is made of Lebanon's democratic façade in contrast to the military governments of other Arab countries. But, at least from the point of view of development, Lebanon's "repressive tolerance", to use Marcuse's term, seems to be at least as damaging as Egypt's totalitarianism.

The choice of the nine Arab countries covered by this study (Libya, Egypt and Sudan in Africa, Syria, Lebanon, Jordan, Iraq, Kuwait and Saudi Arabia in Asia) was not arbitrary. Other Arab countries have been excluded either because of their even more scarce data, as is the case of the two Yemens and the smaller oil-rich countries of Arabia, or because they have been out of the main stream of post-war political development, as is the case of the three countries of Al-Maghreb. Many of the features found to be common to the selected nine countries are believed, however, to apply to those left out.

Finally I wish to express my gratitude to those who, though unaware of my conclusions and not given a chance to correct my errors, have helped me to write this book. Among them it gives me special pleasure to thank Mrs Hanaa El-Sheikh and Mr Hussein Merghany, for providing

---

be more significant than the measurable ones and that in such cases, therefore, any conclusions reached on the basis of the measurable effects only are unwarranted." (Mishan, E.: *The Costs of Economic Growth*, Staples Press, London, 1967, p. XX.)

me with useful data while working as research assistants at the American University in Cairo, and the Ford Foundation, whose generous Middle East Research Award has relieved me of teaching for one academic year (1971/72) during which most of this book was written.

September, 1972.

CHAPTER ONE

ECONOMIC GROWTH AND IMBALANCES

1. *The Arab Economy 25 Years Ago*

The simplest review of economic and social conditions in Arab countries at the end of the Second World War would have been sufficient to make any attempt at classifying all the nine countries as "underdeveloped" or "traditional" as uninteresting as it would have been misleading. Not only were some of the so-called characteristics of underdeveloped countries inapplicable to some of them, but the differences among them, at that time, were at least as glaring as the similarities. This is just as one might expect in countries where there had been little capital accumulation, limited technological progress and where "the diverse historical heritages (had) not yet been overlaid with the similarities imposed by sustained modern economic growth." [1] In such cases a great variety of economic and social conditions would mainly reflect differences in natural resources as well as in social and political institutions which are themselves largely conditioned by these natural resources.

If the term "traditional society", for example, may have fitted Kuwait or Saudi Arabia it would have seemed a highly inappropriate description of Egypt or Lebanon. But Arab countries also displayed great differences with regard to their economic prospects as they appeared in 1945.

Before oil, which was not commercially produced until 1946, Kuwait was described as deprived of any known ingredient for economic growth. A tribal community relying on the extraction of pearls, fishing, some boat-building and sea-borne trade, the town of Kuwait was no more than "a small Arab sea port with sun-baked adobe structures . . . unpaved streets, an old-fashioned souk and a primitive port for shallow-draft vessels . . ." [2] As yet it had no hospital, budget or constitution.[3] When the first population census was undertaken in 1957 Kuwait could boast of only one chemist and two physicians. Like Saudi Arabia, Kuwait had

---

[1] Kuznets, S.: *Economic Growth and Structure*, Heinemann Educational Books, London, 1966, p. 230.

[2] IBRD: *The Economic Development of Kuwait*, the John Hopkins Press, Baltimore, 1965, p. 28.

[3] Kuwait had her first hospital in 1949, her first budget in 1960 and did not have a constitution until 1962.

not yet come to make a distinction between public revenue and the ruler's private purse and the ruler was still the tribal chieftain combining the responsibility of maintaining law and order with that of tribal hospitality.[4]

Having had longer contact with foreign countries, particularly with Persia and India, the Kuwaitis were, as they still are, more urbanized and more sophisticated than the Saudi Arabians. Saudi Arabia's climate and vast arid desert, while protecting her from ever being effectively colonized have also deprived her for most of her history from contact with foreign cultures. Some writers mention that the only two commodities that were introduced into Saudi Arabia between the beginning of Islam and the beginning of the 20th century, were coffee and firearms.[5] In fact, during these thirteen centuries there was hardly any significant change in economic and social life. Pastoral activities remained the basis of her economy with the income of the bulk of the population rarely exceeding subsistence level. In 1945 the income of the kingdom was less than £ 5 million, mainly from the pilgrim traffic to Mecca and Medina, and even this was unstable and depended on uncontrolable circumstances outside Arabia. During the reign of King Abd El-Aziz Al Saud, which lasted for the entire first half of the century (1902-53), the first newspaper, car and aeroplane were introduced, but at mid century Saudi Arabia was still resisting changes and reforms which other poor countries had long ago taken for granted. The introduction of the telephone proved difficult with the conservative Wahhabi Ulama arguing that the instruments "must be agents of the devil since they could carry the voice so far." [6] When one foreign expert tried to explain to King Abd El-Aziz that the basis of all sound finance was to separate the income of the royal family from that of the state the idea seemed to the king so outrageous that the expert had soon to take his leave.[7] Saudi Arabia had to wait another decade for females to be admitted to school and for slavery to be abolished. As late as 1959 the Prime Minister had to call out the army to open the country's first girls' school against protests of Wahhabi traditionalists, and in 1962 the government announced that it had bought all slaves in the kingdom at a price of £ 1,000 a piece, and had given them their

[4] See Shehab, F.: Kuwait, A Super-Affluent Society, in Thompson, J. and Reischauer, R. (eds.): *Modernization in the Arab World*, Van Nostrand Co., Princeton, New Jersey, 1966, pp. 128-30.

[5] Rentz, G.: *Saudi Arabia: The Islamic Island*, in: *ibid.*, pp. 118-9.

[6] Fisher, S.: *The Middle East, A History*, A. Knope, N.Y., 1959, p. 530.

[7] Van der Meulen, D.: *The Wells of Ibn Saud*, J. Murray, London, 1957, pp. 188-9.

freedom.[8] Yet, whatever Saudi Arabia may have lost by her long isolation her population has thereby retained a degree of homogeneity, reflected in a common language, religion and system of values which many countries might envy. For such homogeneity to have contributed to economic development other ingredients of growth were also required. Some of these were provided by the flow of oil revenue, but with oil, homogeneity and social harmony are being gradually lost.

Close in traditionalism to Kuwait and Saudi Arabia were Libya and Jordan, but in contrast to the high degree of self sufficiency of the former the very existence of Jordan and Libya was largely dependent on outside support. Artificially created by Britain and France after World War I, the existence of Transjordan as an independent unit had hardly any economic justification. The area falling east of the Jordan river is essentially arid, poor in fuel resources as well as in raw materials other than phosphates and the unexploited salts of the Dead Sea. It had too small a population and the mouth of Aqaba was its only access to the sea. Its meagre agricultural resources were both undeveloped and subject to the extreme fluctuations of rainfall. Industry was almost nonexistent, being virtually confined to flour milling, olive processing and weaving. When, in 1948, the eastern part of Palestine was added to Transjordan thus constituting the new Kingdom of Jordan, the population tripled while agricultural land increased by only one third. The pressure of Palestinian refugees most of whom had left their capital and means of livelihood behind, was felt not only on agricultural land but also on housing, health and other services. As a result of the Arab-Israeli war of 1948 Jordan also lost her access to the Palestinian port of Haifa and the coastal region of Palestine on which Jordan depended for the disposal of her surplus vegetables and fruit,[9] while the continuing state of tension with Israel discouraged private investment and made expenditure on defence far beyond Jordan's capacity. Jordan therefore came to be heavily dependent on British and later on American aid. In the early 1950's foreign grants accounted for more than 50% of government receipts and about one third of national income while the entire military establishment was financed by Britain.[10]

---

[8] Holden, D.: *Farewell to Arabia*, Faber & Faber, London, 1966, pp. 135-6.

[9] Over 80% of Transjordan's exports before the 1948 war was either sold to Palestine or exported through Haifa (Mazur, M.: Economic Development of Jordan, in: Cooper, Ch. and Alexander, S. (eds.): *Economic Development and Population Growth in the Middle East*, American Elsevier, N.Y., 1972, p. 211).

[10] IBRD: *The Economic Development of Jordan*, Oxford University Press, London, 1957, p. 27; Mazur, *op. cit.*, and Harris, G.: *Jordan, its People, its Society, its Culture*, Grove Press, N.Y., 1958, p. 14.

To call Libya at the end of the war an underdeveloped country would have been rather flattering. Libya seemed not to deserve the term in the sense in which it could be used to describe North America or Australia in the 18th and 19th centuries. A population of no more than a million may have seemed tiny for a country of 1.75 million square kilometres and yet a U.N. mission considering Libya's resources at the time was inclined to regard it as "overdeveloped" in the sense of having already exhausted her meagre resources.[11] As late as 1958, but before oil was discovered, Libya was taken as a good reference point for comparison with other countries for being at the bottom of the range of income and resources.[12] Poor in industrial raw materials and skilled labour and with almost no indigenous entrepreneurship capital accumulation was said to be zero or even negative if account is taken of the destruction caused by the war and the uneconomic use of land. Possibilities for agricultural expansion seemed at the time severely limited and it was uncertain how far the extension of irrigated land would reduce the water resources of that which was already irrigated. B. Higgins described Libya's economy as "deficitary" referring to her continuous deficit in the balance of payment, in the budget of each of the three provinces, in the operation of the power plant in Tripoli as well as of the railways and the harbour.[13] For three decades after Italian occupation these deficits were met by the Italians, then by the two administrating powers: Britain and France and after Libya's independence in 1951 were covered by both foreign aid and leases of military bases. In the year (1958) just preceding the discovery of oil Libya received in official donations 214% of the value of all her merchandise exports, amounting to $ 25 per capita [14] and Higgins wrote that "if Libya was to be brought to a stage of sustained growth, there is hope for every country in the world." [15]

If of our nine Arab countries Libya was at the bottom of the scale Lebanon was at the top.

When per capita income in the other Arab countries was no more than $ 100 per annum, and in four of them less than $ 50 Lebanon's per

---

[11] U.N.: Technical Assistance Programme: *The Economic and Social Development of Libya*, N.Y., 1953, p. 6.

[12] Higgins, B.: *Economic Development*, Norton, N.Y., 1959, p. 26.

[13] *Ibid.*, pp. 28-9.

[14] The corresponding figures for Jordan, but including the flow of some private short-term capital were 799% and $ 45 respectively in the same year. (U.N.: *International Flow of Long-Term Capital and Official Donations (1951-59)*, 1961, pp. 28-9)

[15] Higgins, *op. cit.*, p. 37.

capita income was estimated at $ 140 (1949).[16] Among the Arab countries Lebanon had the lowest mortality and birth rates, the highest share of manufacturing in national income (12% in 1951),[17] the highest rates of literacy and urbanization, the highest number of physicians per capita as well as the most advanced road system.[18] Lebanon's relative prosperity was not new. At the beginning of the century Beirut had already been the main commercial centre for goods passing to and from Lebanon, Syria, Palestine, Northern Iraq and Southern Turkey. Her exports of new silk had been flourishing and the large outflow of Lebanese emigrants were either sending or bringing back to Lebanon their accumulated savings and skill. By the end of the second world war these three factors had considerably declined in importance. The mulberry trees which fed the silk worm had already been cut down for timber during World War I, and after the war increasing foreign competition, as well as the development of rayon, put an end to the silk industry. Migration was facing increasing restrictions from the receiving countries. In 1950 Beirut was also to suffer as a trading centre as a result of the break-up of the economic union with Syria. The Lebanese have, however, characteristically responded well to the challenge. Mulberry trees were replaced by fruit trees which generated far greater income, and tourist attractions were promoted including the building up of a wide network of roads. Also typically Lebanon realized some important gains from the Arab-Israeli war of 1948. Much of the trade which used to pass through Palestine, and particularly through Haifa now turned to Beirut. Sidon and Tripoli, rather than Haifa were to become the terminal of the pipelines carrying oil from Saudi Arabia and Iraq. Like Jordan, Lebanon had to receive her share of Palestinian refugees, but many of them brought to Lebanon large sums of capital. Later on, Lebanon was again to benefit from the

[16] Estimates of per capita income in American dollars in 1949 were: Lebanon 140, Egypt and Syria 100, Iraq 85 and Jordan (1950) 93. An estimate of less than $ 50 was made for the Sudan for 1956. For Kuwait one source mentions $ 21 at the end of the war and another mentions $ 35 as the average income of a skilled labourer (at pre-war prices) before oil started to flow in commercial quantities (1946) and another source mentions $ 25 for Libya. (U.N., Department of Economic Affairs: *Review of Economic Conditions in the Middle East*, 1951, p. 12; Berger, M.: *The Arab World To-day*, Anchor Books, 1962, pp. 200-1; U.N.: *Structure and Growth of Selected African Economics*, (mimeo.), 1958, p. 149; El-Mallakh, R.: *Economic Development and Regional Cooperation: Kuwait*, The University of Chicago Press, Chicago, 1968, p. 6; Shehab, F., *op. cit.*, p. 129 and Higgins, B., *op. cit.*, p. 8)

[17] U.N.: *Yearbook of National Accounts Statistics*, 1958.

[18] U.N.: *Statistical Yearbook*, 1951 and *Review of Economic Conditions in the Middle East*, 1950.

flow of capital from the oil-rich countries as well as from other Arab countries turning "socialist".

What is perhaps the most distinguishing economic feature of the remaining four countries: Sudan, Iraq, Syria and Egypt, when compared with the five already discussed is the former countries' relative richness in agricultural resources. Among these four no one had gone as far as Egypt in exploiting its agricultural resources, but nor had any of the nine such a degree of population pressure on agricultural land. Per capita cultivated land in Egypt was about half that of Lebanon, one fourth that of Jordan and about one tenth of that in Iraq and Syria.[19] In this respect Egypt more nearly resembled such countries as India or China whose overpopulation was the result of their very success in developing their agricultural resources to support a large population *before* their population started to grow at high rates. In the early 1950's R. Nurkse could therefore write that "the highest estimate of the degree of disguised unemployment that I have seen . . . are for Egypt." [20]

While in Egypt one could speak of the marginal productivity of agricultural labour as being close to zero,[21] the marginal productivity of land in the Sudan and Iraq seemed negligible, in the sense that a loss of some of the cultivated land would hardly have affected agricultural production.

Sudan was, however, to stand out among the four "agricultural countries" as the country with the lowest share of industrial output in total product, the least developed infrastructure, the poorest in skilled labour and management as well as the lowest level of education and health.

---

[19] Compared with no more than 388,000 hectares of cultivable land estimated for Lebanon in the early 1950's and 945,000 for Jordan, there were 3,495,000 in Egypt and about double this amount in each of Iraq and Syria while an estimate of 48 million hectares of cultivable land was made for the Sudan. (U.N.: *Economic Development in the Middle East, 1945-54*, N.Y., 1955, pp. 93-4 & 181; U.N.: *Review of Economic Conditions in the Middle East*, N.Y., 1951, p. 69 and 1951-2, p. 16; Burns, N.: *Middle East Economic Problems* (mimeo.), John Hopkins University, 1951, Ch. 6 and Fawzi, S.: *Some Aspects of the Sudanese Economy*, Institute of Arab Studies, (Arabic), Cairo, 1958, p. 21)

[20] Nurkse, R.: *Problems of Capital Formation in Underdeveloped Countries* (1953), Oxford University Press, N.Y., 1966, p. 35.

[21] The very existence of disguised unemployment in Egypt was later doubted, though at least not for the 1930's, by Bent Hansen especially on the basis of more recent data which indicated that earlier estimates of disguised unemployment (ranging from 40% to 50% of the agricultural labour force) had underestimated the substantial amount of non-field and non-agricultural work performed by the peasants. (See Hansen, B. and Marzouk, G.: *Development and Economic Policy in the U.A.R.*, North-Holland, Amsterdam, 1965, pp. 60-4 and Hansen, B.: Employment and Wages in Rural Egypt, *American Economic Review*, June 1969)

Of all the nine countries, Egypt, Iraq and Syria seemed to have the brightest prospects for industrial development. In addition to Lebanon, these three countries emerged from the war with the most developed infrastructure, but they, and particularly Egypt, had the advantage over Lebanon of having a larger population, while Syria and Iraq had a much greater potential in agriculture. If Syria with her relatively small population and poorly developed transport system [22] still lacked a market wide enough to allow the establishment of large-scale industries, this was hopefully to be overcome by her forming, with other Arab countries, a wider economic bloc in which Lebanon was soon to show little interest.

In the three of them, as well as in Lebanon, the war had led to the accumulation of large sums of capital which were either difficult to spend during the war years or were owed to them by Britain and France.[23] The war had also given a big boost to their industries by providing them with a protection which again Lebanon was soon to discontinue. In the late 1940's the rate of gross domestic savings to GNP in Egypt and that of gross investment in Iraq was no less than one tenth, while Syria was investing a percentage of GNP as high as 13-14%.[24] The output of industry and electricity grew by as much as 46% between 1945 and 1950 in Egypt and by about 150% in three years in Iraq (1948/9-51/2) while Syria's output of cotton yarn and rayon was, in 1953, nine to ten times its prewar level and that of textiles about seven times.[25] But of all the nine countries Iraq was the one which promised to grow fastest. Despite having a lower per capita income than Egypt and Syria, Iraq seemed to lack nothing of what was then considered the most important conditions for rapid growth. Compared with Egypt, Iraq had abundance of cultivable land and her oil revenue was to relieve her from capital shortage. In 1950 Iraq was producing less oil than Kuwait or Saudi

---

[22] At the outbreak of World War II the French gave to Turkey the North-Western corner of Syria which resulted in breaking Syria's railway system into three segments connected only through Turkey and Lebanon (Hansen, B.: *Economic Development in Syria*, Rand Corporation, 1969, p. 6 & pp. 39-40).

[23] Britain was indebted by £ 430 million to Egypt and £ 57.9 million to Iraq in 1946 and 1947 respectively and France was indebted to Syria by 10,204 million Francs by January 1948 (U.N.: *Economic Development in the Middle East, 1945-54*, p. 92 & 197 and Shafei, Z.: *Introduction to Money and Banking*, (Arabic), Cairo, 1964, p. 151).

[24] Hansen and Marzouk, *op. cit.*, p. 324; Jalal, F.: *The Role of Government in the Industrialization of Iraq*, London, 1972, pp. 6-7 and IBRD: *The Economic Development of Syria*, John Hopkins Press, Baltimore, 1955, p. 22.

[25] Hansen, B. and Marzouk, G., *op. cit.*, 1965, pp. 64; U.N.: *Economic Development in the Middle East* (1945-54), p. 99 and IBRD, *op. cit.*, p. 21.

Arabia but in the following three years her oil production was to increase four times while she suffered neither from the smallness of population as did Kuwait nor was her infrastructure as backward as that of Saudi Arabia. Little wonder that referring to the economic prospects of Iraq, a British report of the early 1950's stated that

> "granting wise administration, peace and stability, Iraq has a prospect of a rapid advance in national prosperity and individual welfare which has been rarely equalled in history." [26]

2. *Economic Growth*

Looking at the nine countries as a whole one is struck by the degree to which they were favoured, relatively to other underdeveloped countries, by conditions that either should or seemed to be conducive to rapid economic advance.

Twenty years ago they had all achieved political independence except Kuwait and the Sudan. The Sudan has now (1972) been independent for sixteen years and Kuwait for eleven. Most of them were on the whole more favourably situated with regard to economic and social infrastructure than most other underdeveloped countries, especially when compared to the rest of Africa. With regard to the pressure of population on economic resources they were much better situated than the rest of Asia. Their population was relatively homogeneous and relatively little afflicted with class or tribal divisions. In terms of per capita income they started higher up the scale than most countries in south-east Asia and sub-Saharan Africa. Two decades have passed since Egypt started her "revolution" [27] of which one main target was to achieve rapid economic development. Syria started her revolutions three years earlier and although Iraq's revolution came relatively late, Iraq had already started preparing development plans before any other Arab country and most of her oil revenue was assigned for development as early as 1952.[28]

During the two decades following the war (1946-64) the oil producing together with the oil-transit Arab countries, which exclude only the Sudan, received more than $ 13 billion in oil revenues in addition to about $ 2.5

---

[26] Lord Salter's Report "Development of Iraq", quoted in Bullard, R.: *The Middle East, A Political and Economic Survey*, Royal Institute of International Affairs, London, 1958, p. 257.

[27] In spite of obvious objections to the use of this term in describing changes in Arab regimes the term has become so much a part of Arab political jargon that it will be reluctantly retained throughout this essay.

[28] 70% was so assigned in Iraq in 1952 and in Libya in 1958. Half of Saudi Arabia's oil revenue was also allocated to development in 1962.

billion in wages and local purchases by the oil companies.[29] They have received a larger amount of aid per capita than probably any other area in the world. During the same period U.S. economic aid together with the aid commitments of the Sino-Soviet bloc to the nine countries totalled more than $ 3.6 billion.[30] To Egypt alone went no less than one fifth of the total credit commitments of the Soviet Union to all countries between 1954 and 1966,[31] and Jordan's receipts of official aid have been one of

Table 1

Long-Term Economic Aid

(Million U.S. $)

From / *To*	*U.S.A. (July 1, 1945 - June 30, 1964)*	*All D.A.C.* [a] *Countries and Multilateral Agencies (Net Official Receipts only) (1964-69)*	*Sino-Soviet Bloc Commitments*		
			1954-64	*65-69*	*1954-69*
Kuwait	—	- 20.2	—	—	—
Saudi Arabia	46.6	- 31.6	—	—	—
Iraq	46.3	55.6	217	270	487
Libya	205.3	11.6 b	—	—	—
Egypt	943.1	231.9 b	1282	452	1734
Sudan	81.4	107.1 b	22	27	49
Syria	81.9	47.0	231	275	506
Jordan	431.6	284.0 (b)	—	—	—
Lebanon	78.9	65.6	—	—	—
Total	1915.1		1752	1024	2776

[a] Development Assistance Committee of the OECD which includes U.S., Canada, Western Europe and Japan.

[b] 1965-69.

(—) Nil or negligible quantities.

Sources: OECD: *Development Assistance*, 1968 Review, p. 271; 1969 Review, pp. 170-1 and 1970 Review, pp. 194-5; U.N.: *The External Financing of Economic Development, 1962-66*, N.Y. 1968, pp. 16-7; *1964-68*, N.Y. 1970, pp. 45-6; and U.N., Economic and Social Council: *Financing Economic Development of the Developing Countries*, 1969, June 1970, (mimeo.), pp. 13-4; and Remba, O., *op. cit.*, p. 84.

[29] Remba, O.: *Basic Conflicts of Economic Development in the Middle East*, in: Thompson J. & Reischauer, R. (eds.), *op. cit.*, p. 83.

[30] See Table 1.

[31] Tansky, L.: *U.S. and U.S.S.R. Aid to Developing Countries*, Praeger, 1967 , pp. 18-19. Data on actual disbursements as distinct from commitments are not available but the ratio between them has been estimated to be about 40%. Soviet military aid was estimated to be five times greater than economic aid. (See Issawi, Charles: Growth and Structural Change in the Middle East, *Middle East Journal*, Summer, 1971, pp. 310-1 and Vatikiotis, P.: *Conflict in the Middle East*, Allen & Unwin, London, 1971 p. 125).

the highest in the world both in absolute value per capita [32] and as a percentage of GDP. [33]

Population did grow at accelerating rates but in this respect they were not in a worse position than most countries in Asia and Latin America.[34]

Table 2

Population Estimates (1970), Crude Death and Birth Rates, and Natural Rates of Population Growth (1960-65)

Country	Population Estimates on 1 January, 1970 (1000)	Birth Rate	Death Rate	Natural Rate of Population Growth (%)
		Per 1000 of Population		
Kuwait	648	52	14	3.8
Saudi Arabia	5,074	50 [a]	23 [a]	2.7 [a]
Iraq	9,519	48	20	2.8
Libya	1,904	46	18	2.8
Egypt	33,306	42	16	2.6
Sudan	15,389	49	21	2.8
Syria	6,137	48	18	3.0
Jordan	2,238	47	16	3.1
Lebanon	2,614	40	11	2.9

[a] Estimates for 1965-70.

Sources: UNESOB: *Studies on Selected Development Problems in Various Countries in the Middle East*, 1970, p. 73 and U.N., Department of Economic and Social Affairs: *A Concise Summary of World Population Situation in 1970*, pp. 34-5.

[32] The annual net official flow of aid to Jordan (both bilateral and multilateral) amounted on average (1964-67) to $ 32 per capita which was the highest in the world after Israel (44) and New Guinea (38). The total flow of external long-term capital and donations into Jordan in 1967-68 was on average $ 76 per capita, which was second only to Israel (106). (Pearson, L.: *Partners in Development*, Praeger Paperbacks, 1969, p. 393 and U.N.: *The External Financing of Economic Development* (*1964-68*), N.Y., 1970, p. 67).

[33] The average for 1964-67 was 14.8% of G.D.P. which was surpassed only by Loas, New Guinea and South Vietnam (Pearson, *op. cit.*).

[34] The three stages through which, according to Arthur Lewis, the rate of population growth tends to pass if the birth rate remains more or less constant at about 40 per thousand, seem roughly to have been applied to the Arab world. The first stage in which the death rate tends to decline from about 40 to 30 per thousand and population therefore increases by about 1% seems to have characterized the Arab countries before the second world war. The further decline of the death rate from about 30 to 20 per thousand as a result of the application of modern medical facilities occurred in most Arab countries during and just after the war, when the rate of population growth rose to about 2% largely as a result of the introduction by Britain and her allies of large-scale modern drugs and insecticides to protect the health of their soldiers. During the

During the past two decades Arab countries have in fact shown some impressive rates of growth, and in spite of rapid population growth, real per capita income rose in most of them at an average annual rate of more than 2%. Not only the oil countries but also Jordan achieved much higher rates of growth than the average rate for underdeveloped countries. During the period 1953-68 Iraq had a regular growth rate of real GDP of 6 to 7% per annum.[35] During the 1960's Kuwait realized an average annual rate of growth of 7 to 8%,[36] and Saudi Arabia an even higher rate [37] while Libya's rate of growth was the highest in the world.[38] Also remarkable was the growth rate of Jordan which, counter to pessimistic expectations, surpassed that of oil-rich Iraq.[39]

Although such high growth rates were not achieved by other Arab countries, each of them, with the exception of the Sudan, whose performance was the least impressive,[40] passed through some periods during

---

1960's with a birth rate ranging between 40 per thousand in Lebanon and 52 in Kuwait, and a death rate ranging between 11 in Lebanon to 21 in the Sudan, Arab population has been growing at about 3% annually. (see Table 2) While this rate is the same as that of Lewis' third stage it cannot be said for most Arab countries that medical facilities are now available to most individuals all over the country as Lewis assumes to happen in this stage. The growth rate of about 3% has therefore been realized because *both* birth and death rates have been considerably higher than those assumed by Lewis. (See Lewis, A.: *The Theory of Economic Growth*, Allen & Unwin, London, 1957, pp. 306-7; Hurewitz, J.: *The Politics of Rapid Population Growth*, in Thompson & Reischauer (eds.), *op. cit.*, p. 88 and Remba, *op. cit.*, p. 62).

[35] U.N.: *Yearbook of National Accounts Statistics*, 1969.

[36] El-Mallakh, *op. cit.*, p. 7.

[37] E. Asfour estimated the average annual real rate of growth of Saudi Arabia's GNP to be 6% for 1954/5 - 60/1, 11% for 1960/1 - 64/5 and 8% for 1964-67 (*Prospects and Problems of Economic Development of Saudi Arabia, Kuwait and the Gulf Principalities*, in Cooper & Alexander (eds.), *op. cit.*, p. 371. See also UNESOB: *Selected Developments Problems*, 1968, p. 26).

[38] After a sluggish growth in both agriculture and industry accompanied by a severe inflation during the 1950's Libya's real domestic product grew, thanks to oil, at the fantastic rate of 21.6% per annum and real per capita income at 17.3% between 1960 and 1970 (OECD: *Development Assistance*, 1971 Review, p. 117).

[39] Jordan's GDP at current market prices grew at an average rate of over 10% between 1954 and 1966 which is one of the highest in the world, even after allowing for a 2% rate of increase in prices. (Mazur, *op. cit.*, p. 215).

[40] During the first four years following independence (1956-60) the annual real growth rate of the modern sector in the Sudan was about 5%. Since the traditional sector is estimated to contribute about 45% of GDP and was growing during the same period at about 3.3% annually the whole economy would have been growing at about 4.2%. With a rate of population growth of about 2.8% real per capita income would have been growing at only about 1.4%. This last rate declined to less than 1% in the following six years (1960-66) giving Sudan one of the lowest rates of growth in Africa. An estimate made for the whole decade (1960-70) gives the real rate of growth of

which growth was fairly rapid and considerably above that of underdeveloped countries as a whole. This occurred in Syria during the decade following the second world war,[41] in Egypt between 1956 and 1963 [42] and in Lebanon after the 1958 civil war.[43]

Rates of industrialization were also considerably higher than those of underdeveloped countries taken as a whole. The rate of growth of manufacturing was as high as 16% per annum in Jordan (1959-66) and 11.3% in Saudi Arabia (1962-68) with comparable rates in all of them except Syria.[44]

Table 3

Average Annual Rates of Growth of Real GNP at Factor Cost (1960-67) and Per Capita GNP (1967)

Average Annual Growth Rates (1960-1967)	*Per Capita GNP in U.S. $ in* 1967				
	100 -	200 -	300 -	400 -	500 *or more*
More than 6%		Jordan	S.Arabia		Kuwait
					Libya
5-6%	Egypt	Iraq Syria			
4-5%					Lebanon
3-4%	Sudan				

Sources: Pearson, L.: *Partners in Development*, Report of the Commission on International Development, Praeger Paperback, N.Y., 1969, supplemented and modified by other sources referred to above.

---

the whole economy as 4.1% and that of real per capita income as only 1.2%. (See: U.N.: *Survey of Economic Conditions in Africa - 1968*, N.Y., 1972, p. 16; OECD: *Development Assistance*, 1971 Review, Dec. 1971, p. 117 and Wynn, R.: The Sudan's 10-year Plan of Economic Development 1961/62 - 1970/71: An Analysis of Achievement to 1967/68, *Journal of Developing Areas*, July 1971, pp. 557 & 563-4).

[41] During which the Syrian economy grew at 5 to 6% per year. (See Hansen, B.: *Economic Development in Syria, op. cit.*, p. V. and IBRD: *The Economic Development of Syria, op. cit.*, pp. 20-1).

[42] After a virtual long-term stagnation of Egypt's real per capita income for about half a century and until the mid-1950's, it increased between 1956/7 and 1962/3 at more than 3% annually. (Hansen & Marzouk, *op. cit.*, p. 4).

[43] Lebanon's average annual rates of growth at current prices were estimated at 5.3%, (NDP, 1950-57); at 9.5% (GDP, 1957-64) and at 7.4% (NDP, 1964-68). (See UNESOB: *La Croissance Économique et le Niveau de Qualification de la Population Active dans Divers Pays du Moyen-Orient* (mimeo.), Beirut, April 1971, p. 102).

[44] See Table 5.

Table 4

Per Capita GNP in U.S. $ in 1968

Kuwait [a]	3474	Jordan	260
Libya	1020	Syria	210
Lebanon	560	Egypt	170
Saudi Arabia [a]	311	Sudan	100
Iraq	260		

[a] 1967/68.

Sources: U.N.: *Yearbook of National Accounts Statistics*, 1969 and OECD: *Development Assistance*, 1971 Review, pp. 154-5.

Table 5

Average Annual Rates of Growth of Manufacturing Output at Factor Cost at Constant Prices

Country	*Period*	%
Underdeveloped Market Economics	1950-60	6.7
	1960-68	6.2
Libya	1962-68	11.0
Kuwait	1966-68	11.1
Saudi Arabia	1962-68	11.3
Iraq	1953-60	14.1
	1960-68	4.6
	1953-68	8.8
Syria	1956-68	4.8 [a]
Jordan	1959-68	13.9 [a b]
Lebanon	1957-68	10.3
Egypt	1957-67	9.3 [a]
Sudan	1955-60	6.2
	1960-64	10.7
	1955-64	8.2

[a] Includes mining, quarrying, electricity, gas and water in addition to manufacturing.
[b] At current prices.

Sources: U.N.: *Yearbook of National Accounts Statistics*, 1968 & 1969; Hansen, B.: *The Economic Development of Syria*, *op. cit.*, p. 11 and UNESOB: *La Croissance Économique*, *op. cit.*, p. 57.

It was presumably on the basis of such figures that one writer has recently stated that "the Middle Eastern countries should, on the whole be viewed as examples of past development success." [45] This is indeed highly doubtful. The high rates of growth in the four oil countries have been mostly the reflection of the rapid growth in oil production. Their

[45] Cooper, Charles, in Cooper & Alexander (eds.), *op. cit.*, p. 4.

Table 6

Oil Revenues (Million Dollars)
(1961-70)

Year	*Kuwait*	*Saudi Arabia*	*Iraq*	*Libya*
1961	464.3	400.2	265.5	3.2
1962	526.3	451.1	266.6	38.5
1963	556.7	502.1	325.1	108.8
1964	655.0	651.0	353.1	197.4
1965	671.1	655.2	374.9	371.0
1966	707.2	776.9	394.2	476.0
1967	717.6	852.1	361.2	631.0
1968	765.6	965.5	476.2	952.0
1969	812.2	1008.0	483.5	1132.0
1970	896.5	1200.3	513.3	1294.8

Source: The World of Oil, Arabic Weekly, Beirut, 18 Sept. 1971, p. 5.

ranking with regard to the rate of growth of the whole economy has therefore followed closely their ranking in the rate of growth of oil production.

Between 1961 and 1970 the annual oil revenues accruing to Iraq and Kuwait almost doubled, those of Saudi Arabia tripled, while Libya with a population not exceeding one fifth that of Iraq, received in oil revenues in 1970 slightly less than those received by Iraq and Kuwait combined.[46]

In spite of the rapid increase in per capita income and in manufacturing production, serious economic and social imbalances continue to exist in all the nine countries, and in many cases tend to be intensified. Their failure to face these weaknesses has been only slightly covered up in the oil-rich countries by the continuing increase in oil revenue, from which Lebanon has also greatly benefitted, and in Egypt and Jordan by the large flow of foreign aid. The two countries which were not in either respect so fortunate have either shown poor economic performance all through the last two decades, as we have seen for the Sudan, or suffered a prolonged economic setback, as was the case in Syria.[47]

[46] By 1970 Libya had emerged as the biggest Arab oil exporter and realized the highest revenue from oil among the Middle Eastern countries (see table 6 and The Economist Intelligence Unit: *Quarterly Economic Review, Oil in the Middle East*, No. 1, 1972, pp. 6-7 & 15).

[47] Syria's rapid growth during the post-war years was followed by twelve years (1956-68) during which the annual compound growth rate at constant 1963 factor cost was no more than 4.2% compared with 5% to 6% during the previous decade. Per capita real income grew therefore at only 1% compared with about 3% between 1945 and 1956. In fact, according to Hansen, if the growth of defence is disregarded per capita income in the period 1956-68 would have probably fallen. (Hansen, B.: *Economic Development in Syria, op. cit.*, p. V, 11 and 16).

3. *Economic Structure*

In spite of a clear tendency for the share of agriculture in total output to decline, in most cases quite heavily,[48] manufacturing still makes a modest contribution to national income, except in Egypt. In 1951 the highest share of manufacturing in GDP (that of Lebanon) was 12% compared with about 9% for Egypt. By 1968 Egypt had more than doubled this proportion while, among the rest, the highest share was only 13%, and it was as low as 2% in Libya and Saudi Arabia,[49] compared with 17% and 18% for such underdeveloped countries as India, Chile or Colombia. In some cases the share of manufacturing in GDP hardly increased at all, as in Saudi Arabia, where this share has remained at about 2% since 1963,[50] and in Syria and Lebanon, where it remained at 12% to 13% over a much longer period (1953-67), while in Libya it showed a heavy decline. In Iraq, after a remarkable rate of growth of manufacturing in the 1950's (14% annually between 1953 and 1960) it declined to less than one third of this rate between 1960 and 1968 and thus the share of manufacturing in GNP remained virtually constant at about 9% between 1959 and 1968.[51] The general decline in the share of agriculture was therefore mainly in favour, not of manufacturing, but either of oil, as in Libya, or of construction and services as in most of the rest.[52]

But apart from the small contribution of manufacturing to total output, its growth, even where its share in output has been rising, has contributed little to the development of other sectors. This was partly the result of the small proportion of capital goods in total manufacturing output, of the small proportion of manufacturing in total exports and of the small proportion of labour engaged in manufacturing to the total labour force.

a. By far the greatest part of Arab manufacturing still consists of the processing of agricultural goods for consumption. Food, beverages, tobacco, textiles and wearing apparel industries, taken all together, account for more than 50 to 70% of total Arab manufacturing output

---

[48] See Tables 7 & 8.

[49] See Table 9.

[50] Economist Intelligence Unit: *Saudi Arabia and Jordan*, No. 1, 1971, p. 6.

[51] U.N.: *Yearbook of National Accounts Statistics*, 1969.

[52] This was nowhere as conspicuous as in Syria where as much as two thirds of the increase in the value added between 1956 and 1968 occurred in the service sector. In Lebanon while the share of manufacturing remained virtually constant that of services rose, between 1953 and 1968 from 63 to 70%, perhaps the highest in the world. (See Hansen, B.: *Economic Development in Syria*, p. V, and Table 8).

Table 7

Development of Sectoral Distribution of GDP in three Oil-Producing Countries (Percentages)

			Industry			
Country	*Year*	*Agriculture* [a]	*Mining and Quarrying*	*Other* [b]	*Services*	*Total GDP*
Iraq	1953	22	40	10	28	100
	1958	19	36	14	31	100
	1964	19	35	12	34	100
	1968	19	34	14	33	100
Libya	1958	27	7	12	54	100
	1964	7	52	3	38	100
	1968	3	61	8	28	100
Saudi Arabia	1962/3	10	44	13	33	100
	1968/9	6	46	15	33	100

[a] Includes agriculture, forestry, hunting and fishing.
[b] Includes manufacturing, electricity, gas and construction.
Sources: U.N.: *Yearbook of National Accounts Statistics*, 1969 and UNESOB: *La Croissance Économique*, *op. cit.*, p. 127.

while another 6 to 8% consists of furniture, wood, paper, printing and publishing.[53] Interindustrial relationships have therefore been of such an elementary kind as the sale of fruits to the fruit processing industry or of leather to the shoe industry . . . etc.[54] In countries such as Kuwait and Saudi Arabia where agriculture was less able to provide much of the required raw materials, a good part of manufacturing consisted of such activities as water distillation, the manufacture of salt, printing and publishing, etc. In these two countries, as well as in Libya and Iraq, the establishment of industries based on petroleum and natural gas, either as raw materials or as sources of power, has been far too slow in spite of the recommendations made long ago by international missions or by foreign experts for the establishment of petrochemical and fertilizer

[53] U.N.: *Report of the Symposium on Industrial Development in Arab Countries*, N.Y., 1967, p. 2.

[54] For an elaboration of this point for Egypt, see Mabro, R. and O'Brien, P.: Structural Changes in the Egyptian Economy, 1937-65 in Cook, M.A. (ed.): *Studies in the Economic History of the Middle East*, Oxford University Press, London, 1970, pp. 418-9. See also Mazur, *op. cit.*, p. 220 and Owen, R.: The Economic Aspects of Revolution in the Middle East, in: Vatikiotis, P. (ed.): *Revolution in the Middle East*, Allen & Unwin, London, 1972.

Table 8

Development of Sectoral Distribution of GDP in the Non-Oil Countries (Percentages)

Country	*Year*	*Agri-culture* [a]	*Industry* — *Manufacturing Mining Quarrying Electricity Gas and Water*	*Industry* — *Con-struc-tion*	*Industry* — *Total In-dustry*	*Services*	*Total GDP*
Egypt	1952	41	9	3	12	47	100
	1960	30	22	3	25	45	100
	1968/9	28	23	5	28	44	100
Jordan	1954	30	9	3	12	58	100
	1960	16	9	5	14	70	100
	1968	16	13	6	19	65	100
Syria	1953	44	12	3	15	41	100
	1963	36	13	4	17	47	100
	1969	24	14	4	18	58	100
Lebanon	1953	19	14	4	18	63	100
	1966	11	15	6	21	68	100
	1968	10	15	5	20	70	100
Sudan	1955	60	5	6	11	29	100
	1958	58	5	7	12	30	100
	1964	54	7	6	13	33	100

[a] Includes agriculture, forestry, hunting and fishing.

Sources: U.N.: *Yearbook of National Accounts Statistics*, 1969; The Pearson Report, *op. cit.*, pp. 362-3; National Bank of Egypt: *Economic Bulletin*, 1970, No. 4; UNESOB: *La Croissance Économique, op. cit.*, p. 17; Federation of Arab Chambers of Commerce, Industry and Agriculture: *Arab Economic Development, 1950-65*, (Arabic), Beirut, 1967, pp. 11 & 311, and Economist Intelligence Unit: *Syria, Lebanon and Cyprus*, Annual Supplement, 1971, p. 5.

industries. As far back as 1952, for example, the World Bank mission to Iraq suggested the construction of a chemical plant at the oil fields in Kirkuk to utilize the natural gas. In 1956 the Little report on Iraq stated that the establishment of rayon and paper industries and recovering sulphur from natural gas were economically justified. In 1965, when these and other industries had already been included in Iraq's development plans for more than ten years many of them were still under consideration.[55] In the same year a little less than two thirds of Saudi Arabia's

[55] Jalal, F., *op. cit.*, pp. 33, 36 & 42.

Table 9

Sectoral Structure of GDP at Factor Cost
(In Million of National Currencies and Percentages)

Sector	Egypt [a] 1968/9 £.E.	%	Libya [b] 1968 £.L.	%	Sudan [b] 1964 £.s.	%	S. Arabia [c] 1966/7 Riyal	%	Kuwait [c] 1966/7 K.D.	%	Iraq [d] 1968 I.D.	%	Jordan [e] 1968 J.D.	%	Lebanon [f] 1968 £.L.	%	Syria [g] 1969 £.S.	%
Agriculture	601.5	28	22	3	238.2	54	1007	8	11	0.5	187	19	27.5	16	436	10	1182	24
Mining and Quarrying	461.8	21	515	61	0.3	—	6926	53	1376	61.1	329	34	20.0	12	552	13	702 [l]	14
Manu-facturing			19	2	24.5	6	250	2	81	3.6	86	9						
Construction	105.5	5	53	6	25.4	6	535	4	106	4.7	29	3	9.8	6	194	5	191	4
Electricity, Gas & Water	36.6	2	3	—	2.3	1	252	2	52	2.3	16	2	2.3	1	99	2		
Transport, Storage and Com-munication	115.2	5	30	4	62.7	14	900	7	63	2.8	64	7	14.5	9	380	9	481	10
Wholesale and Retail Trade	198.9	9	53	6			932	7	214 [i]	9.5	59	6	29.1	18	1360	32	783	16
Banking, Insurance and Real Estate			10	1	3.6	1	50	—			15	1	3.0	1	164	4	141	3
Ownership of Dwellings	115.3	5	40	5	11.6	3	494	4			15	1	12.3	7	235	6	377	8

Table 9 (*continued*)

Public Administration and Defence } Services	533.2	25	56	7	45.1	10	1113	8	128	5.7	115	12	33.2	20	357	9	706	14
Services			39	5	24.9	6	643	5	221 [k]	9.8	50	6	15.5	9	397	10	364	8
GDP at Factor Cost (h)	2177	100	840	100	438.6	100	13102	100	2252	100	975	100	167.2	100	4174	100	4927	100

[a] GNP at 1959/60 prices
[b] at 1964 prices
[c] at current prices
[d] at 1966 prices
[e] at current prices
[f] at 1968 prices
[g] NNP at 1963 prices
[h] percentages may not add up to 100 because of rounding
(—) less than .5%
[i] excludes real estate
[k] includes real estate
[l] includes electricity, gas and water.

Sources: U.N.: *Yearbook of National Accounts Statistics*, 1969; UNESOB: *La Croissance Économique, op. cit.*, p. 276; National Bank of Egypt: *Economic Bulletin*, 1970, No. 4; Economist Intelligence Unit: *Syria, Lebanon and Cyprus*, Annual Supplement, 1971, p. 5 and El-Mallakh, R.: *op. cit.*, pp. 125-7.

natural gas was being flared, the rest being used mainly either as fuel for the petroleum industry itself or reinjected into the oil fields.

b. In all the nine countries except Egypt, manufactured exports contribute at present less than one tenth of all current receipts of foreign exchange. Even in a field as obvious for the oil producing countries as exporting refined petroleum little progress has been made, so that in no Arab country does the proportion of refined to crude-oil production exceed one fifth at present. Egypt was the only country in which the share of manufactured exports in total commodity exports rose significantly [56] even though they still consist mainly of such items as textiles, dried onions, processed fruits and vegetables and shoes, while others rely heavily on imported inputs. The corresponding share for Lebanon was even higher than that of Egypt in the late 1960's but Lebanon had already, in the mid-1950's been in the unique position among the Arab countries of having more than one third of her commodity exports consisting of manufactured goods, and the corresponding proportion in the late 1960's was no higher.[57] Moreover, as a contributer to total foreign-exchange receipts Lebanon's manufacturing is much less important, the foreign exchange brought to Lebanon by tourism alone being more than that brought by all her commodity exports (excluding re-exports).[58]

But apart from manufacturing, Arab countries have made little progress even in diversifying their exports of primary products. The oil countries remain virtually as dependent on oil, and Syria and Sudan on cotton as they were two decades ago.[59]

---

[56] This share rose from 11% in 1950 to 17% in 1959, 21% in 1965 and 29% in 1968/9 (National Bank of Egypt: *Economic Bulletin*, various numbers).

[57] 32% in 1967-69 compared with 35% in 1954-56 (U.N.: *Yearbook of International Trade Statistics, 1958 and 1969*).

[58] UNESOB: *Studies on Selected Development Problems*, 1970, p. 18.

[59] In *Kuwait* the share of oil in the total value of exports remained at between 97% and 98% during 1958-65 while most of her non-oil exports are re-exports. In *Saudi-Arabia* the share of oil declined only slightly from 99.9% in 1954-5 to 97% in 1967. In *Iraq* this share *increased* from 88% (1953-5) to 93.4% (1965-7), and her exports, other than oil, hardly increased at all between 1953 and 1969. In *Libya* the share of oil continued to rise during the 1960's reaching 99.9% in 1969, while the quantity index of non-oil exports *declined* by about 30% between 1962 and 1967. In *Syria* the share of raw cotton in total exports was 37.4% in 1953-5 and 41.0% in 1967-9. In the *Sudan* cotton together with gum arabic, sesame and cotton seed still account for over 80% of total exports.

Some progress was achieved, however, by Egypt and Jordan. As a result of the expansion of *Egypt's* exports of other agricultural products such as rice, onions and groundnuts as well as some manufactured goods, the share of exports of raw cotton in total exports declined from 86% in 1950 to 55% in 1965 and to an average of 43% in 1968-9 The proportion of vegetables and fruits in *Jordan's* exports declined from *c.* Available data on the distribution of labour among the various sectors is often out-of-date, [60] but there is enough evidence to suggest that the share of labour engaged in manufacturing in the economically active population cannot, at present, be higher than 11% in any Arab country, while in Saudi Arabia, Sudan and Libya it is considerably lower.[61] Even in Egypt the increasing share of manufacturing in GDP was far from being reflected in a similar change in the structure of the labour force. Out of an increase in total labour force of about 800,000 persons between 1960 and 1965 manufacturing absorbed only one fourth, while services absorbed more than half the increase.[62] During the same period the share of manufacturing in the total labour force therefore rose from 10% to only 11% and it is unlikely that this share would have risen since then. This could be partly explained of course by the rapid growth of the population, but it was also due to the tendency to favour capital intensive techniques.[63]

In none of the oil-producing countries does the oil-industry occupy more than 4% of the total active population,[64] as a result of its high capital intensity and the low rate of refining, transportation and marketing of oil within these countries' borders.[65] In 1957 the percentage was

---

44% in 1954-5 to 35% in 1966-7, while her exports of phosphates, which were non-existent in the early 1950's, constituted 26% of total exports in 1968-9 It is worth noting however, that Jordan's exports of tomatoes and phosphates alone constitute no less than 55% of the total value of exports.

Thanks to the relative diversity of her climate and topography, with a relatively high level of humidity on the coast, the dry climate of the Behaâ valley, and the low temperature of the mountain, *Lebanon* has always been in the favourable position where no one primary commodity constituted more than 15% of all commodity exports.

[60] See Table 10.

[61] Iraq's available data on the size and distribution of the labour force is as old as 1957 but the number of persons employed in manufacturing was estimated at 152,000 in 1967, or no more than 1.7% of total population. (Republic of Iraq: *Statistical Handbook*, *1957-67*, Bagdad, 1968, p. 88).

[62] See Mabro, R.: Industrial Growth, Agricultural Underemployment and the Lewis Model: The Egyptian case, 1937-65, *Journal of Development Studies*, July 1967, p. 333. Commenting on this the same writer says that what happened in Egypt was therefore not as much a reallocation of labour in favour of manufacturing as "a transfer of underemployment from one economic sector to another."

[63] See *ibid.*, p. 341 where Mabro points out that the capital/labour ratio in Egyptian manufacturing rose by 116% between 1947 and 1965 and that between 1952 and 1958, while no increase in employment occurred in the 'modern sector', capital intensity in establishments of 10 workers and more seem to have increased by 40%. See also Wahba, J.: *Surplus Labour and the Choice of Techniques in Egypt*, unpublished M.Sc. thesis, The American University in Cairo, 1971.

[64] See Table 10.

[65] It is estimated that it takes roughly 3.5 times as many man-days to produce a ton of refined oil products as a ton of crude oil (Issawi, Charles and Yaganeh, M.: *The Economics of Middle Eastern oil*, Faber & Faber, London, 1962, pp. 150-1).

Table 10

Distribution of Economically Active Population by Sector (Percentages)

		Secondary [b]					
			of which				
Country	Primary [a]	Total	Manufacturing	Mining and Quarrying	Tertiary [c]	Activities not Adequately Described + Unemployed	All Sectors
Libya (1964)	36	20	7.2	3.5	32.3	11.7	100
Iraq (1957)	47.9	14.8	9.5	0.2	24.3	13.0	100
S. Arabia [d] (1963)	58 [f]	8	3	2	22	12	100
Kuwait (1965)	1	32.9	9.7	3.8	62.8	3.3	100
Lebanon [e] (1968)	34	21	...	...	45	—	100
Egypt (1964/5)	52	16	11		32	—	100
Jordan (1961)	35.3	21.5	8.4	2.4	24.8	18.4	100
Syria (1967)	58.1	13.7	9.0	0.4	22.9	5.3	100
Sudan (1956)	85.8	5.6	5.0	—	7.3	1.3	100

[a] Agriculture, forestry, hunting and fishing.
[b] Manufacturing, mining, quarrying, electricity, gas, sanitary services and construction.
[c] Commerce, transport, storage, communication and other services.
[d] Estimate, in which all public sector has been included in the tertiary sector.
[e] Estimate.
[f] Includes an estimated 20% nomads.
(...) not available.

Sources: I.L.O.: *Yearbook of Labour Statistics*, 1969; UNESOB: *La Croissance Économique*, *op. cit.*, pp. 84-5 & 229; U.A.R. Central Agency for Public Mobilization and Statistics: *Statistical Indicators*, Cairo, July 1966, p. 25.

no more than 0.2% in Iraq and it is probably lower now since, as the oil industry matures, it tends to employ less labour in *absolute* terms. It is interesting to note that Egypt's oil industry employed in the mid-1960's more than the number employed by the same industry in any of the Arab oil-rich countries and that Egypt's textile factory employment alone employed more labour than the total employment in the oil industry of all Arab countries combined.[66] It is also worth noting that a not insignificant proportion of those employed by the oil industry are foreigners, especially in the higher ranks.[67]

[66] See Sayegh, K.: *Oil and Arab Regional Development*, Praeger, N.Y., 1968, p. 302 and Issawi and Yaganeh, *op. cit.*, pp. 150-1.

[67] In Saudi Arabia foreigners constitute over one tenth of total employment in the oil industry.

Table 11

Labour Productivity [a] *in Manufacturing and Agriculture*
(Dollars per Labourer)

Country	*Year*	(1) *Manufacturing*	(2) *Agriculture*	(3) *Ratio* (1) : (2)
S. Arabia	1962/3	1563	601	2.60
Iraq	1958	719	273	2.63
Jordan	1961	588	514	1.14
Kuwait	1966/7	4684	6230	0.75
Lebanon	1968	2021	618	3.27
Syria	1960	639	347	1.84
	1967	700	285	2.46

[a] Domestic product of each sector divided by the number of economically active in the same sector.
Source: UNESOB: *La Croissance Économique*, *op. cit.*, p. 59.

It follows that the two most productive sectors, manufacturing and oil, nowhere occupy more than 15% of the economically active population, while the two sectors which still occupy by far the greatest part of labour are those where low productivity and disguised unemployment are most in evidence: agriculture and services.[68]

The persistent predominance of the service sector as a contributor to GDP (together with oil) and as a source of employment (together with agriculture) is of course nothing unusual for underdeveloped countries. Professor Kuznets has shown that the average share of services in GNP could be a little less than 50% in countries with per capita income of less than $ 200 annually and that its share at this level of income is higher than its share in countries with per capita income of $ 575 or more.[69] In the Arab world, as in other underdeveloped countries, the main reason is the relatively few employment opportunities elsewhere.

[68] For the relative productivity of labour in agriculture and manufacturing see Table 11. As for oil, if one assumes that 80% of the total number employed by the oil industry are engaged in crude production the average quantity of oil produced per worker could reach 5800 tons per year. The highest level of productivity in the oil sector is that of Kuwait with about 18,000 tons per worker per year. (See Sayegh, K., *op. cit.*, p. 87).

[69] The average shares of the service sector in GNP in 59 countries in 1958 were as follows:

	Per Capita GNP ($)			
	100-199	*200-349*	*350-574*	*575 or more*
% of services in GNP:	45.6	43.2	51.3	43.7

(Kuznets, S.: *Modern Economic Growth*, Yale University Press, 1966, pp. 402-3.)

However, in Jordan, Syria and particularly in Lebanon [70] the share of services in GDP is distinctly higher than the corresponding average share in other countries with the same per capita income. One must therefore look for reasons other than the usual one of the limited employment opportunities in agriculture, industry and mining. Among these are the relatively large defence establishments in Jordan and Syria, the high relative importance of tourism in Lebanon and Jordan, of financial services in Lebanon and of the government sector in Syria, the influx of the Palestinian refugees who found little employment opportunities in the commodity sectors, and what appears to be a special talent for acting as middlemen, especially among the Lebanese.

In Lebanon an unusually high proportion of the output of the service sector is sold to foreigners.[71] An increase in the demand for services in Lebanon is, therefore, to that extent, a reflection of rising incomes outside rather than within Lebanon. The Lebanese economy will also, to the same extent, remain vulnerable to economic and political fluctuations outside its borders. Moreover, foreign demand for Lebanon's services is of high elasticity and highly sensitive to policy moves taken by neighbouring countries, such as the restriction on travel to Lebanon, or the closing of borders between Syria and Jordan. At the same time, Lebanon's ability to retaliate is quite limited since other Arab countries are less dependent on Lebanon as a market for their exports than Lebanon is on them.[72]

---

[70] One writer has estimated that in Beirut there is one merchandise retail store for approximately every 125 persons, and another mentions as a conservative estimate that about 60% of Beirut's ground floor is in commercial or industrial use. (Eid, N.: Merchandise Retailing in Lebanon, *Middle East Economic Papers*, 1969, p. 21 and UNESOB: *Environmental Implications of Urban Settlements: Issues of Urban Ecology in the Middle East*, Beirut, 1971, (mimeo.), p. 11).

[71] As much as 36% of the output of the Lebanese service sector in 1965 was estimated to have been sold to non-residents. The corresponding percentage for transport and communications was 20%, housing 25%, tourism 65% and imports 33%. (See Sayigh, Y. and Atallah, M.: *A Second Look at the Lebanese Economy*, Dar Al-Taliaa, Beirut, 1966 (Arabic), pp. 16-26). According to another estimate almost one third of Lebanon's total personal income during 1961-65 could be attributed to tourists' expenditure, transport of goods and persons *across boundaries* (excluding purely internal transport), transit, entrepot and triangular trade, emigrant remittances and capital transfers, all of which are largely governed by factors beyond Lebanon's control. (See Badre, A.: *Economic Development of Lebanon*, in Cooper & Alexander (eds.), *op. cit.*, p. 191).

[72] See Khalaf, N.: Economic Size and Stability of the Lebanese Economy, *Middle East Economic Papers*, 1967, p. 72. On the effect of trade on Lebanese morality, Professor Y. Sayigh writes: "In this trade-centred society, cleverness enjoys a premium over creativity. The emphasis on gains made through clever bargaining is greater than the emphasis on steady business relations and on deals based on the respective merits

4. *The Balance of Payments*

Taken as a whole, total exports of Arab countries have been rising at a rate considerably higher than that of underdeveloped countries. This has been partly due to the high rates of growth of the exports of Lebanon and Jordan (which in Jordan's case is almost exclusively due to phosphates), but was mainly due, of course, to the rapid increase in international demand for oil. If oil was excluded the average rate would fall below that of underdeveloped countries taken as a whole.[73] Thus, while the oil countries continue to realise a big and increasing surplus in their balance of trade and, with the exception of Iraq,[74] also in their balance of current accounts, all the non-oil countries continue to realize trade deficits.[75] The deficit is relatively small in the Sudan, and if the proceeds from invisible trade in the case of Syria (mainly from oil-transit and tourism) are added, the deficit declines heavily and may in some years turn into a small surplus. The most serious trade deficits are, therefore, those of Lebanon, Egypt and Jordan.

Lebanon's increasing trade deficit is turned into a surplus by invisible exports (mainly transit trade and tourism) and by the flow of private capital, especially from the oil countries. But the dependence of Lebanon's balance of payment on the inflow of private capital is at least as precarious as her dependence on trade and tourism. In the first place, most of the inflow of capital into Lebanon (about two thirds in 1964-5) [76] consists of short-term bank liabilities which can be withdrawn on demand. Secondly, a good part of capital movements consists of emigrants' remittances as well as flight capital from other Arab countries. While the former is dependent both on the number of Lebanese emigrants admitted by

---

of the goods exchanged. And the search for a quick turnover and large easy profits accentuates an inclination to speculative enterprise and militates against sustained effort and long-term investment promising long-term though low profit rates." (*Entrepreneurs of Lebanon*, Harvard University Press, Cambridge, Massachusetts, 1962, p. 11).

[73] During 1960-67 the average annual rates of growth of the value of commodity exports were as follows: Libya 90%, Lebanon 15.3%, Jordan 16%, Saudi Arabia 11.6%, Kuwait 5.6%, Iraq 5%, Egypt 1.9% and Sudan 1.6% (*Pearson's Report, op. cit.*, p. 369).

[74] Though a trade-surplus country, Iraq has a balance of trade which has been much less favourable than those of the other oil countries. During 1960-67 the rate of increase in her exports was not much higher than the average rate for underdeveloped countries as a whole (5% and 4% respectively) and in contrast to the other three oil countries her surplus on the balance of current account sometimes declines to quite a low level or turns into a deficit.

[75] See Table 12.

[76] Azhari, N.: *L'Evolution du Système Economique Libanais*, L.G.D.J., Paris, 1970, p. 63. See also Khalaf, N., *op. cit.*, pp. 72-3.

foreign countries and the degree of their continued attachment to Lebanon, the latter could decline if Lebanon's political or financial stability is threatened, or alternatively, if the political climate or investment opportunities in other Arab countries improve. The oil-rich countries may also discover one day that it is more profitable in the long-term to invest more of their surplus revenue at home or directly in Western Europe or the U.S. without passing through Lebanese banks as intermediaries. This was clearly shown by the repercussions of the Intra Bank crisis of 1966 and of the June war in the following year.[77]

In both Egypt and Jordan the surplus on invisibles (mainly the Suez Canal in Egypt and tourism in Jordan) normally covers no more than one third of the trade deficit, and for the rest they both rely mainly on foreign aid. In place of a regular, though small, trade surplus which Egypt used to realize before World War II, a trade deficit came to be the normal feature of her balance of payments and went on increasing until it reached £E. 110 million in 1965. It was reported that in the following year the government had to sell one-third of the gold reserves to pay for current imports.[78] In Jordan, despite the high rate of increase in exports, imports rose so much faster that her trade deficit multiplied more than 6 times between 1950 and 1966. By 1967 Egypt and Jordan came to have

---

[77] Largely as a result of the rise in U.S. and European interest rates in the second half of 1966 to levels which had never been reached since the early 1920's, the Lebanese banking system faced a sudden rise in the demand for foreign currencies and was put under strong pressure to increase its purchases of foreign funds. The big drain on the banks' reserves in high-powered money brought the ratio of reserves to demand deposits from a peak of 13% in May to a low of 10% in September 1966, a fall of 23%. The situation was made worse by the usual practice of several Lebanese banks of holding long-term claims in unsafe proportions, by the traditionally liberal attitude of the Lebanese system towards reserves and by the absence of defined legal reserve ratios. All this culminated in the collapse of the Intra Bank, the largest commercial bank in Lebanon, in October 1966, which was followed by a flight of capital out of Lebanon and a painful fall in the deposits held by local banks. Lebanon's image of financial security was again impaired by the June War, by the Israeli raid of Beirut airport in 1968 and by the border clashes between Israel and the Palestinian guerillas. While in 1966 the net inflow of capital to Lebanon was £L. 355 million, in 1967 it fell to £L. 97 million, making Lebanon unable, for the first time, to cover her deficit on current account. A balance-of-payment deficit of £L. 1.9 million was thus realized in 1967 compared with a surplus of £L. 96.5 million in the previous year. The situation would have been much worse if the same events had not also caused a heavy decline in imports and hence in the trade deficit. (On the Intra affair see: Ghattas, E.: Lebanon's Financial Crisis in 1966, A Systemic Approach, *Middle East Journal*, Winter 1971; Azhari, *op. cit.*, pp. 93-4; Badre in Cooper & Alexander (eds.), *op. cit.*, p. 204 and Sayigh and Attallah, *op. cit.*)

[78] Kanovsky, E.: *The Economic Impact of the Six-Day War*, Praeger, N.Y., 1970, p. 253.

two of the highest external public debts per capita among the underdeveloped countries. They were also among the worst situated with regard to the ratio of public external debt to commodity exports [79] and in Egypt's case, with regard to the ratio of service charges on public debt to export earnings.[80]

Table 12

Balance of Trade and Export-Import Ratios
(Annual Averages)

	Balance of Trade (Millions of National Currencies)			*Export-Import Ratios* [a]		
	1954-5	1963-4	1968-9	1954-5	1963-4	1968-9
Kuwait	135 [b]	344	360 [c]	400 [a]	398	294 [b]
S. Arabia	1507	3691	5731	378	391	324
Libya	—9	76	485	33	176	305
Iraq	95	159	221	215	224	247
Sudan	—3	—24	—7	93	75	92
Lebanon	—327	—705	—1134	22	21	30
Syria	134	—200	—557	134	77	57
Egypt	—31	—176	14	82	57	105
Jordan	—21	—45	—48	12	14	23

[a] Commodity exports as a percentage of commodity imports.
[b] Average 1958-9.
[c] Average 1966-7.
Sources: Calculated from U.N.: *Yearbook of International Trade Statistics*, 1969; UNESOB: *Studies on Selected Development Problems*, 1970, pp. 14-7 and El-Mallakh, *op. cit.*, p. 24.

Oil producing or not, all the nine countries except Syria are food-deficit countries. This applies even to Iraq and the Sudan, the richest two countries in agricultural resources relatively to population. Iraq's food imports are now equal to the value of all her non-oil exports, while Jordan's *net* imports of foodstuffs were greater in 1966-68 than all her exports put together. With the change in rainfall Syria alternates between being a food-surplus and a food-deficit country and when the deficit

[79] Sudan's burden of external debt is much lower. Compared with a per capita external public debt of about $ 60 for each of Egypt and Jordan on the 1st January, 1968, that of the Sudan was about $ 20. Again, compared with a ratio of total external public debt to the value of commodity exports in 1967 of more than 3 in both Egypt and Jordan it was between 1 and 1.5 in the Sudan. (U.N.: *The External Financing of Economic Development (1963-67)*, N.Y., 1969, pp. 111-3).

[80] In 1967 Egypt debt-service payments absorbed about one third of her export earnings compared with about one fifth in the case of India and Pakistan. Only four out of 68 countries for which data is available (namely Argentina, Tunisia, Brazil and Mexico) had higher ratios than that of Egypt. (*Ibid.*, p. 115).

does occur it is usually small. Her food surplus, however, has been decreasing.[81]

Yet, available data on food consumption, which is presumably more reliable and hides a smaller degree of inequality than per capita income figures, shows that in the mid-1960's the average diet was still deficient. With regard to quantity only in Egypt and Syria did calorie intake exceed requirements, but in most cases the deficiency was not great. As for quality, physiologists recommend a daily intake of total protein per head of 1 g./kg of body weight for adults and 2 to 4 times as much for infants and children. Half of this amount is recommended to be of animal origin.[82] Table (14) shows that in at least seven countries the requirements of total protein were met but not that of animal protein.[83]

5. *Arab Economic Integration*

Over the last two decades Arab statesmen as well as Arab economists rarely missed a chance of referring to the advantages that could be realized from Arab economic integration. Until 1964, however, Arab countries could only achieve the conclusion of preferential trade and payments agreements, mainly bilateral, which had very limited effect on the size and structure of inter-Arab trade. The exemption from customs duties included in these agreements applied mainly to agricultural commodities which had either already been exempt from customs duties before the agreement, or had been subject to negligible tariffs. The fact that virtually all the agreements were of only one-year duration discouraged private entrepreneurs from drawing their investment plans on the basis of a market wider than that of their own country.[84] Annexes were often added to the agreements including long lists of products to which the exemption from tariffs would not apply, while the agreements were usually silent with regard to the exemption from import licenses, quantitative and foreign exchange restrictions. The whole agreement was in any case liable to be ignored once the political relations between the

---

[81] See Table 13.

[82] Amin, G.: *Food Supply and Economic Development, with Special Reference to Egypt*, Cass, London, 1966, p. 58.

[83] It is worth noting that in Egypt, for whom food consumption data exists for a relatively long period, the quality of the average diet as measured by the intake of animal protein seems to have remained remarkably unchanged since the late 1940's although total protein intake indicates some improvement (FAO: *Production Yearbook*, 1970).

[84] Diab, M.: *Inter-Arab Economic Co-operation, 1951-60*, Economic Research Institute, American University of Beirut, 1963, p. 88.

Table 13

Food [a] *Imports and Exports*

Country	*Period (annual Averages)*	*Total Imports*	*Imports of Food and Live Animals*	*% of Imports of Food and Live Animals to Total Imports*	*Exports of Food and Live Animals*	*Food and Live Animal Deficit*
Jordan (mill. Dinars)	1954-5	24	8	33.3	1	7
	1966-7	62	16	25.8	4	12
Sudan (mill. £S.)	1954-5	49	13	26.5	4	9
	1968-9	91	14	15.4	8	6
Iraq (mill. ID.)	1954-5	85	15	17.6	14	1
	1968-9	151	22	14.6	9	13
Kuwait (mill. KD.)	1968-9	224	35	15.6	3	32
Syria (mill. £S.)	1954-5	387	52	13.4	175	—123 [c]
	1968-9	1281	224	17.5	238	—14 [c]
Lebanon (mill. £L.)	1954-5	429	141	32.9	51	90
	1967-8	1621	357	22.0	153	204
Libya [b] (mill. £L.)	1955-6	15	4	26.7	1.05	3
	1968-9	236	29	12.3	.05	29
Egypt [b] (mill. £E.)	1955-6	184	24	13.0	15	9
	1967-8	317	96	30.3	54	42
S. Arabia (mill. SR.)	1966-7	2235	679	30.4	8	671

[a] Unless otherwise stated includes also beverages and tobacco.
[b] Does not include beverages and tobacco.
[c] Food and live animal surplus.

Sources: U.N.: *Yearbook of International Trade Statistics* 1958 & 69 and Kingdom of Saudi Arabia, Ministry of Finance and National Economy: *Statistical Yearbook*, 1969.

Table 14

Calorie and Protein Intake (1964-66)
(per capita per day)

Country	*Calorie Intake (number)*	*Calorie Requirement (number)*	*Calorie Intake as % of Requirement*	*Total Protein Intake (grams)*	*Requirement of Total Protein (grams)*	*Total Protein Intake as % of Requirement*	*Intake of Animal Protein*
Lebanon	2360	2425	97	70	57	123	20
S. Arabia	2080	2225	93	56	50	112	9
Sudan [a]	2090	2185	96	59	59	100	19
Syria	2450	2390	102	69	63	109	12
Egypt	2960	2380	124	76	64	119 [b]	11 [b]
Jordan	2400	2425	99	65	64	102	11
Iraq [c]	2050	2245	91	59	55	107	14
Libya	2540	...	...	64	...	...	18

[a] Data relate to area covering 87% of the population.
[b] Provisional data for 1966-67.
[c] Provisional.
(...) Not available.

Sources: Actual intake from FAO: *Production Yearbook*, 1970, requirements from Stickley, S. & others (eds.): *Man, Food and Agriculture in the Middle East*, American University of Beirut, 1969, p. 23.

two parties became strained. Thus between 1951-3 and 1962-3 the share of inter-Arab in total Arab trade increased only slightly, and in some cases as those of Jordan, Lebanon and Syria, it even declined.[85] The main exception during this period was the big increase in the trade between Egypt and Syria during their union (1958-61) whereby Syria's imports from Egypt in 1961 was more than five times their level in 1957.[86]

In 1964 an agreement was reached between five Arab countries: Syria, Iraq, Kuwait, Jordan and Egypt to establish an "Arab Common Market". Two more countries later signed the agreement: Yemen in 1967 and the Sudan in 1969. On paper the agreement was extremely ambitious. Obviously imitating the European Economic Community, it aimed not only at the removal of trade barriers but at the ultimate establishment of a common tariff vis-à-vis the outside world, the free movement of labour and capital, a uniform agricultural, industrial, commercial and monetary

[85] See UNESOB: *Studies on Selected Development Problems*, 1967, p. 16 and Al-Ghandour, A.: *Arab Economic Integration*, (Arabic), Institute of Arab Studies, Cairo, 1970, pp. 110-123.

[86] Kanovsky, E.: Arab Economic Unity, *Middle East Journal*, Spring 1967, p. 215.

policy ... etc. The agreement came into force on 1st January, 1965, but in July of the same year Kuwait's National Assembly voted to withdraw and later the Sudan was permitted to delay the implementation of the agreement until the beginning of 1972 and Yemen to become merely "an observer".[87] Only four countries therefore are now bound by the agreement: Iraq, Syria, Jordan and Egypt.[88] All the four countries continued, however, to apply quota restrictions, so that the Arab League's Economic Unity Council had officially to recognize their right to do so, merely obliging the country "forced by its circumstances to apply quota restrictions to give preference to the products of other member countries within the country's own productive and export capacities".[89]

Table 15 shows that the share of trade between the four countries in their total trade has risen quite rapidly after 1964 but that this share is still very low especially with regard to imports. For obvious reasons these

Table 15

Share of Intra-A.C.M. In the Total Trade of Arab Common Market Countries (Percentages) [a]
1958-1969

Year	*Exports*	*Imports*
1958	5.1	3.5
1959	8.8	4.7
1960	6.7	3.7
1961	8.0	3.9
1962	3.7	1.8
1963	4.2	2.4
1964	3.8	2.0
1965	3.4	2.0
1966	4.5	2.1
1967	4.3	2.2
1968	5.9	3.2
1969	6.2	3.9

[a] Value of exports/imports of Iraq, Syria, Jordan and Egypt to each other as a percentage of their total exports/imports.

Source: UNESOB: *Étude Comparative des Cadres Institutionnels du Commerce Intra-Marche Commun Arab*, (mimeo.), June 1971, Tables 16 & 17.

[87] *Al-Ahram*, 17.3.1971.

[88] Lists of goods were submitted by these countries requesting their exemption from the elimination of customs duties. These requests were later withdrawn except for some of Jordan's (*ibid.*).

[89] The Council's decision no. 251, 6.11.1966, quoted by Al-Ghandour, *op. cit.*, p. 123.

countries rely more on each other in disposing of their exports than in acquiring what they need of consumer or capital goods. Between 1960-64 and 1965-69 the total five-year value of the imports of the four countries increased by $ 989 million of which only 22 million was due to the increase in intra-Arab Common Market trade compared with an increase of 251 million in their imports from the E.E.C. countries and of 942 million from the Sino-Soviet bloc.[90]

But even with regard to exports, it is unlikely that the removal of trade barriers will, by itself, increase the ratio of inter-Arab to total Arab exports beyond a modest level. As long as Arab exports continue to consist mainly of primary commodities they will continue to rely on the markets of industrial countries. Moreover, their reliance on the importation of capital and consumer goods from these countries will tend to favour the directing of these primary exports to them, as is the case at present.[91] In fact, given the existing structure of production in Arab countries, an operative customs union may prove disadvantageous to most of them, a fact which helps to explain their laxity in bringing it into effect. While an effective Arab customs union is of little use to the oil countries, as an outlet for their oil exports, these countries would have to replace their imports of Western goods by inferior Arab products. The oil countries may rightly fear that they would in fact be subsidizing other Arab countries suffering from foreign-exchange shortages while others, particularly Jordan, could fear the loss of customs duties which constitute the government's main source of revenue. For all except the most industrially advanced, the gain from a more efficient reallocation

[90] UNESOB: *Étude Comparative des Cadres Institutionnels du Commerce Intra-Marché Commun Arab*, (mimeo.), June 1971, pp. 18-9.

[91] Partly because the structure of their exports has shown little change but also for political reasons, Arab countries continue to rely heavily on the market of one or a few countries. Thus, while the exports of Egypt and Syria are now heavily oriented towards the Soviet Union, most of the oil exports go to Western Europe and Japan. The change in the destination of Egypt's and Syria's exports since the mid-1950's resulted not in the diversification of their export markets as much as in replacing one predominant market by another. While in 1948, 29% of all Egyptian exports went to Britain and another 24% to other West European countries and only 13% to Eastern Europe, in 1968/9 the shares were reversed to 49% to Eastern Europe (mainly the Soviet Union) and China, and 21% to all of Western Europe including Britain. Similarly, while Syria exported almost nothing to the socialist countries in 1953, their share rose to 41% in 1964. In both cases, exports to the Eastern bloc consist mainly of cotton.

Of the nine Arab countries, only Jordan, Syria and Lebanon export a high proportion of their total exports to other Arab countries, the average for 1968/9 being 69%, 60% and 35% respectively. (U.N.: *Yearbook of International Trade Statistics*, 1969).

of existing industries is likely to be small when compared with the likely increase in unemployment, especially if one is to consider the scarcity of capital in many of them and the difficulties of retraining labour and providing economic and social facilities for new industries. It is difficult to imagine, or indeed to justify, that Syria or the Sudan should close down some of their textile factories and tolerate more unemployment simply because the Egyptian textile factories are more efficient. Even if the liberalization of trade increases total and per capita income in each of the Arab countries, the less-developed among them may still give their lower rate of industrial growth a greater weight than the increase in their total income.[92] The danger of polarization is further aggravated by the fact that the distances between the levels of industrial development and infrastructure in Arab countries are far greater than those existing between any two members of EEC or EFTA. All this is presented not as an argument against the liberalization of Arab trade but merely to point out its insufficiency. The real advantages of economic integration among underdeveloped countries stem not from the freeing of largely non-existing trade but from its promotion, from its role in promoting new industries rather than in allowing a more efficient allocation of existing ones. Such an aim would require that co-operation should extend to the sphere of production and investment, to the establishment of mutually complementary industries which would be distributed among member countries in accordance with their resource endowments.[93] Only through such co-ordination could the disadvantages just referred to be avoided or outweighed by greater benefits. Thus, while a common external tariff could by itself only harm Lebanese traders, it could, if coupled with a common Arab development policy, be beneficial to Lebanon's industrial and agricultural expansion. Similarly, while a wider Arab market may bring little benefit to oil exports, it may be a necessary condition for the expansion of petro-chemical industries. Most Arab governments, however, have shown little inclination to relegate part of their power to a common authority or to sacrifice the economic interests of strong minorities for the sake of long-term industrial growth. No attempt was

---

[92] For an elaboration of this point see Andic, F., Andic, S. and Dosser, D.: *A Theory of Economic Integration for Developing Countries*, Allen & Unwin, London, 1971, pp. 17-8.

[93] See: Kitamura, H.: Economic Theory and the Economic Integration of Underdeveloped Regions, in Wionczek, M. (ed.): *Latin American Economic Integration*, Praeger, N.Y., 1966, p. 57 and Mikesell, R., The Theory of Common Markets and Developing Countries, in Robson, P. (ed.): *International Economic Integration*, Penguin Books, 1971, p. 174.

therefore made to harmonize Arab development plans in such a way as to avoid unnecessary duplication. When Iraq, Kuwait and Saudi Arabia, for example, recently embarked on establishing petro-chemical and fertilizer plants, no attempt was made to co-ordinate their plans in this field so that each of them is likely to face the competition of the other two in their efforts to market their output. All of them, however, continue to pay lip service to the cause of economic integration and, in order to pacify the Arab nationalists among their subjects, formally adhere to largely ineffective agreements.

It is indeed ironic that the only examples of genuine economic integration between Arab countries, other than that which accompanied the political union between Egypt and Syria (1958-61) have been imposed upon Arab countries by a foreign power. Such, for example, were the customs union among most Arab countries which lasted between 1870 and 1914 under the Ottoman Empire, or the Middle East Supply Centre which co-ordinated their production and trade under British domination during the second world war, or the customs union between Syria and Lebanon, established by the French administration between the two world wars, which provided protection for Lebanese as well as Syrian manufacturing but was dissolved soon after the two countries achieved their independence.[94]

[94] For a detailed account of these earlier examples see Musrey, A.: *An Arab Common Market: A Study in Inter-Arab Trade Relations*, 1920-67, Praeger, N.Y., 1969.

CHAPTER TWO

THE POLITICS OF SAVING AND INVESTMENT

1. "*Traditional*" *Governments*

One of three conditions given by W. Rostow for the take-off to occur is non-economic. It refers to "the existence, or quick emergence of a political and institutional framework which exploits the impulses to expansion in the modern sector ... and gives to growth an on-going character." [1] Only thus would growth become "self-sustained" and "the country's normal condition." [2] One of these required institutional changes is the rise of a new élite or a new leadership which supersedes the old land-based élite and which regards development as a possible and desirable task. The economic surplus, i.e. income above minimum levels of consumption, could thus be directed not to "country houses, servants, personal ornaments and temples" but towards "roads, railways, schools and factories." [3]

Few facts about the Arab world are better known than the wastes of the traditional governments of the oil-producing countries, particularly Saudi Arabia. Such expenditure was still taking place in Saudi Arabia in the late 1950's when scarcely one productive enterprise was being developed other than the oil fields.[4] Sympathetic writers, including the King's personal friends who wrote on the history of Saudi Arabia, as well as U.N. economic reports, give the impression that this is now past history and that since the 1958 crisis, which brought the country to the verge of bankruptcy,[5]

---

[1] Rostow, W.: *The Stages of Economic Growth*, Cambridge University Press, 1962, p. 39.

[2] *Ibid.*, p. 36.

[3] *Ibid.*, p. 19.

[4] One famous example is King Saud's expenditure of at least £25 million on his new Nasariyeh palace in Riyadh which included "4 separate palaces for his reigning wives, 32 mansions for his scores of concubines and their retinues and 37 villas for various princes as well as royal schools, a hospital, a museum, a zoo and what was said to be the world's largest air-conditioning plant." (Holden, D.: *Farewell to Arabia*, *op. cit.*, p. 119).

[5] In 1958 it was suddenly revealed that the country was spending 25% more than its income and had accumulated foreign debts of some $ 310 million, or as much as the whole of its oil revenue of that year. The value of the Saudi Riyal had dropped by about 50% when control over finances was handed over to Prince Faisal in 1958. A series of monetary reforms followed and royal expenditure was reduced so that Saudi Arabia was able to repay her debts by 1959. (See Sayigh, Y.: Problems and

"the revenue of the state was to be used primarily to promote the interests of the nation as a whole." [6] This view is apparently based on the fact that while allocations for the private purse of the King have been heavily reduced (from 17% of the state budget in 1959 to 5.5% in 1964) [7] allocations for development increased (from 7% of total estimated government outlays in 1960 to 38% in 1967). [8] Similarly, while the average annual rate of growth of gross fixed capital formation was estimated at only 3% between 1954/5 and 1960/1 it rose to as much as 15% in the following four years and to 17% between 1964 and 1967.[9] These figures, however, greatly exaggerate both the development efforts of the government and the reduction of wasteful government expenditure.

According to Professor Sayigh, actual development expenditure of the Saudi government rarely rises, on the average, beyond 50% of allocations, which are politely but vaguely described as "invariably far beyond the capacity of government machinery to utilize." [10] But even if one concentrates on allocations one notices that total allocations to industry and commerce for the whole of seven years (1964-70) amounted to only 85.9 million Riyals [11] compared, for example, with the total estimated cost of 729 million Rials of the two airports planned to be built in Jeddah and Riyadh and which, according to an official report, "would be provided with modern facilities including mobile lounges for passengers".[12] Again, as shown in table (16), allocations for agriculture in the three development budgets of 1967/8 to 1969/70 constituted between 11.1% and 15.4% of total 'development' allocations, and those for industry and commerce no more than 0.3 to 0.6% compared with between 36.3 and 48.5% allocated for "other" expenditures which include "royal household, interior affairs, information, religious affairs, etc." [13] In 1968-9 another economic crisis seems to have occurred in

---

Prospects of Development in the Arabian Peninsula, in Hopwood, E. (ed.): *The Arabian Peninsula*, Allen & Unwin, London, 1972, p. 289, and Holden, *op. cit.*, pp. 119-20).

[6] Rentz, G.: *Saudi Arabia: The Islamic Island*, *op. cit.*, p. 120.

[7] Ismael, T.: *Governments and Politics of the Contemporary Middle East*, The Dorsey Press, Illinois, 1970, p. 373.

[8] UNESOB: *Studies on Selected Development Problems*, 1968, p. 26.

[9] Asfour, E.: *Prospects and Problems of Economic Development of Saudi Arabia, Kuwait and the Gulf Principalities*, *op. cit.*, p. 371.

[10] Sayigh, *op. cit.*, p. 300.

[11] Saudi Arabian Monetary Agency: *Annual Reports* of various years.

[12] Saudi Arabian Monetary Agency: *Annual Report*, 1387-88 A.H., p. 38.

[13] Economist Intelligence Unit: *Saudi Arabia & Jordan*, Annual Supplement, 1971, p. 4.

Table 16

Saudi Arabia: Distribution of Allocations in the Development Budgets (Percentages)

	1967/8	1968/9	1969/70
Transport and Communication	28.0	30.7	26.2
Agriculture	15.0	15.4	11.1
Petroleum and Minerals	1.9	2.2	2.1
Industry and Commerce	0.5	0.6	0.3
Labour and Social Affairs	0.4	0.3	0.3
Education	3.6	2.3	1.5
Health	0.9	0.6	0.5
Municipalities	9.8	11.6	9.5
Others	39.9	36.3	48.5
Total	100.0	100.0	100.0

Sources: Economist Intelligence Unit: *Saudi Arabia & Jordan*, Annual Supplement, 1971, p. 4.

Table 17

Annual Averages of National Savings and Gross Investment (Percentages of GNP)

Country	*Period*	*Savings*	*Investment*
Kuwait	1964-68	45	19
Saudi Arabia	1964-68	45	18
Libya	1960-67	39	25.4
Iraq	1959-64	18.4	17.3
	1964-68	18	17
Egypt	1959/60-64/5	12.7 [a]	16.6 [a]
	1965/66-68/9	13.5	15.2
Syria	1960-65	15.3	16.9
	1964-68	9	12
Jordan	1959-64	—6.0	13.7
	1964-68	1	14
Sudan	1960-64	12.1	14.9
	1960-67	9.8	13.5
Lebanon	1964-68	12	20

[a] Percentage of GDP.

Sources: UNESOB: *Long-Term Prospects in the Development of Selected Countries and Sub-Regions of the Middle East*, (mimeo.), Sept. 1971, p. 53; OECD: *Development Assistance*, 1970 Review, Dec. 1970, pp. 100-1; Gov. of Libya: *Statistical Abstract*, 1968, p. 330; UNESOB: *Studies on Selected Development Problems*, 1967, p. 4; U.N.: *Yearbook of National Accounts Statistics*, 1969; Hansen, B.: Economic Planning in the U.A.R., in Vatikiotis, P. (ed.): *Egypt Since the Revolution*, Allen & Unwin, London, 1968, p. 36 and the Egyptian Ministry of Planning: *Follow-Up and Evaluation of Economic Development in U.A.R. (1965/6-68/9)*.

Saudi Arabia which, though much milder than that of ten years earlier, seems to have also been caused by government overspending. No figures on real rather than budgeted spending and revenues are published but some have estimated that in 1968 and 1969 the government spent more than 500 million Riyals over and above receipts. In the 1970/1 budget allocations for new projects have therefore been reduced to only £20 million.[14]

Similar, though not as glaring, examples of wasteful government expenditure can be quoted for Kuwait and Libya.[15] If the three countries have been saving as much as 39% to 45% of GNP [16] this is simply the result not only of their huge oil revenues but also of the way in which this revenue is obtained, whereby it flows directly into the hands of the governments which are therefore spared the usual difficulties of collecting taxes in a poor society.

Two more Arab governments, those of Jordan and Lebanon could be classified with those of Saudi Arabia, Kuwait and pre-1969 Libya as being "unrevolutionary" or "traditional" in Rostow's sense. In both of them, although there are frequent government changes, power has remained in the hands of a very small number of rich and influential families with strong business interests.[17]

The two countries have two of the lowest rates of saving among the nine countries, with Jordan often realizing a negative rate. While Jordan's gross private saving was sufficient to cover half of gross domestic investment, it was offset by an equally large government deficit, mainly due to heavy defence expenditure, so that during 1959-66 the whole of Jordan's gross domestic investment was financed by foreign aid, as can be seen from Table 18.

Of Lebanon's economic policies, or rather the lack of them, little can be understood without reference to her confessional social structure and particularly to the fact that no single sect constitutes a majority of the population. According to an unwritten National Pact agreed upon in

---

[14] Economist Intelligence Unit: *Saudi Arabia & Jordan*, No. 1, 1971, p. 4.

[15] For Kuwait, for example, the IBRD 1961 mission expressed "some doubts as to the need for what amounts to two airports alongside each other." (IBRD: *The Economic Development of Kuwait*, *op. cit.*, p. 110). For examples on pre-revolutionary Libya see Farley, *Planning Economic Development in Libya*, Praeger, N.Y., 1972, p. 225.

[16] See Table 16.

[17] Of Jordan, M. Mazur writes: "Even the most scrupulous and energetic of ministers finds it difficult to resist the political pressures for excessive government protection and assistance when he has very little information and no clear decision criterion with which to defend a negative position." (*Op. cit.*, p. 270).

Table 18

Jordan: Ratios to Gross Domestic Investment

	Foreign Aid	*Gross Domestic Savings*	*Gross Private Savings*	*Gross Government Savings*
1959-62	1.17	—0.17	0.49	—0.65
1963-66	0.87	0.11	0.53	—0.41
1959-66	1.00	0.00	0.51	—0.51

Source: Mazur, M., *op. cit.*, p. 222.

1943 by the major religious communities and faithfully followed to this day, a precarious balance has to be observed in the distribution of government offices among the various sects, from the Presidency, which has to be occupied by a Maronite, down to the lowest levels of administration.

According to this pact the Lebanese parliament must include six christians to every five non-christians. But since any major policy issue which the parliament may discuss is bound to be met by opposition from some religious or regional group, Lebanon's parliament has very rarely exercised any real political power. In nearly 40 years only one government has fallen because of the loss of parliament's confidence and this occurred as long ago as 1930.[18]

The Cabinet is also constituted on a confessional as well as regional basis so that it normally includes two Sunnis, two Maronites and one each of Greek Catholics, Orthodox, Shiites and Druzes. It is therefore as handicapped as the parliament, but much less stable. "As most Cabinet members come from parliament, a new Cabinet or even a reshuffled one presents hope to an aspiring deputy. Even incumbent ministers, as soon as they sense the weakness of their Cabinet, begin to prepare for their inclusion in the next one by attacking their colleagues in the present one." [19] Little wonder that Lebanon had some 46 Cabinets between 1926 and Feb. 1964, an average of less than eight months per Cabinet.[20]

Political parties do exist in Lebanon but again, largely because of

---

[18] Hurewitz, J.: Lebanese Democracy in its International Setting, in Binder, L. (ed.): *Politics in Lebanon*, J. Wiley, N.Y., 1966, p. 214.

[19] Suleiman, M. W.: *Political Parties in Lebanon*, Cornell University Press, N.Y., 1967, pp. 51-2.

[20] Kerr, M.: *Political Decision Making in a Confessional Democracy*, in Binder, L. (ed.), *op. cit.*, p. 192.

confessional and regional divisions, no party or combination of parties ever obtained a sufficient number of seats in parliament to exert a strong influence on the government. The results of the 1960 and 1964 elections, for example, brought no more than 34 and 28 seats, respectively, to all the eight to ten parties, out of a total of 99 seats. The other seats were held mainly by feudal leaders, landlords and financiers.[21] During a period of 21 years (1943-64) between 42% and 54% of the deputies in the Lebanese parliament were designated "propertied", having no particular profession and living off their land and/or other property (see Table 19).[22] This high proportion of property owners could be partly attributed to the weakness of political parties but is also due to the high candidature fee (3000 LL. in 1964) which is lost to the candidate who gets less than 25% of the district's votes [23] as well as to the high costs of electoral campaigns on which the state puts no limit.

Table 19

Lebanon: Members of the Chamber of Deputies by Occupation (%)

Term in Office	*Propertied*	*Lawyers*	*Doctors*	*Engineers*	*Journalists*	*Business-men*	*Miscellan-eous* [a]	*Total* [b]
1943-47	41.8	34.5	7.3	3.6	—	9.1	3.6	99.9
1947-51	43.6	30.9	10.9	1.8	1.8	10.8		99.8
1951-53	44.2	29.9	6.5	4.0	5.2	10.4		100.2
1953-57	43.2	38.6	4.5	4.5	4.5	4.5		99.8
1957-60	44.0	40.9	4.5	4.5	1.5	1.5	3.0	99.9
1960-64	54.5	28.3	6.1	3.0	2.0	1.0	5.0	99.9

[a] Judges, teachers, pharmacists, economists and ex-government officials.
[b] Total does not add to 100 because of rounding.

Source: Suleiman, M.: *Political Parties in Lebanon*, Cornell University Press, N.Y., 1967, p. 47.

It has been noted that during the 1960 elections the amount of money in circulation increased by LL. 3 million.[24] Political newspapers, of

[21] Suleiman, *op. cit.*, p. XV.

[22] Other deputies included in Table 19 may indeed own land or other property but they differ from those classified as "propertied" in having a profession. (See *ibid.*, p. 47).

[23] *Ibid.*, p. 48.

[24] Geertz, C.: The Integrative Revolution, in Geertz, C. (ed.): *Old Societies and New States*, The Free Press of Glencoe, London, 1963, p. 144. Geertz writes: "Both places on tickets led by strong figures, and votes themselves, are bought ... rivals are slandered and, on occasion, physically attacked; favoritism, nepotism or otherwise is accepted procedure, and spoils are considered the normal rewards of office. 'There is no right in Lebanon', it is said, 'there is only silver and the 'fix'."

which there were no less than 49 daily in 1962,[25] make up for their inevitably low circulation by relying on subsidies provided either by some foreign country with interest in Lebanese politics, or by some interest groups within the country, and it is widely believed that each and every political paper in Lebanon is so subsidized.[26]

The struggle for power in Lebanon pivots in fact on a number of strong personalities who are often absentee landlords or heads of prominent families with a large following, loyal to them personally irrespective of their own or their leaders' ideological commitments. The leaders' aim is simply to manipulate the political system to further their own careers or economic advantage.

"It is paradoxical", writes Professor Malcolm Kerr, "that although the spirit of political controversy reaches everywhere, and the politicians' invasion of the sphere of competence of bureaucrats and magistrates is commonplace, the paralysis of the highest centers of political authority signifies the absence of true politics from the system. There are no political decisions, but only superimpositions by politicians of their own informal criteria of adjudication and administration on to the formal criteria which judges and bureaucrats are nominally supposed to follow. The state has withered away, or rather has remained withered since birth, and the country is left with a (very non-Marxian) 'administration of things'." [27]

This last fact is clearly revealed by an examination of the Lebanese state budget in which the greater part of government expenditure is allocated to ordinary administration with only a very small proportion going to expenditure on infrastructure. In the 1969 budget the traditional functions of government as a "night watchman" represented no less than 40% of total government expenditure. This included the allocation to the Presidency, the Cabinet, and the ministries of justice, foreign affairs, interior and defence.[28] Taxation in Lebanon is still considered merely as a means of collecting sufficient revenue for the state to perform its traditional functions while its role in redistributing income or financing economic development is yet to be recognized. The general income tax has never been adopted, and whenever the need arises for increasing its revenue the Lebanese government almost invariably falls on indirect

[25] In addition to 160 weekly and 99 various monthly magazines. (Suleiman, *op. cit.*, pp. 36-7).

[26] *Ibid.*

[27] Kerr, *op. cit.*, p. 190.

[28] Beydoun, T.: *The Influence of Economic System on Consumer's Behaviour in Lebanon* (Arabic), Social Science Institute, Lebanese University, Beirut, 1970, p. 213 and IFRED: *Le Liban face à Son Developpement*, Beirut, 1963, p. 270.

taxes and particularly on customs duties. The role of customs duties in providing protection for domestic manufacturing or agriculture is at best a secondary consideration. While, for example, some raw materials that compete with local products are exempted from customs duties, others that are not locally produced are subject to duties of 11% or more. On the whole, however, the dominant influence of the merchant class has ensured that hardly any tariff is high enough to be prohibitive.[29] The most recent example of how these interests obstruct any attempt made by the government to implement a tariff policy for the protection of home industries was provided in 1971. In September a decree was passed increasing import duties on 450 luxury items with the proclaimed aim of raising LL. 35 million to finance social and economic projects. This gave rise to such a wave of strikes and protests by merchants, importers and shopkeepers that the government had to capitulate and cancelled the decree in the following month.[30]

With such a liberal importation system only a small proportion of total investment in Lebanon is directed to manufacturing or agriculture. Again, the high proportion of foreign-owned banks and insurance companies [31] has led a considerable proportion of their investment to be directly or indirectly made abroad. Of the capital that flows into Lebanon from the oil countries hardly any goes into the commodity sectors, the bulk of it, as we have seen, taking the form of short-term bank deposits. The relatively small part that goes into long-term investment, has gone mainly to real estate.

2. *The New Elites*

With the beginning of Syria's era of coups-d'état in 1949, the Egyptian coup in 1952, those of Iraq and Sudan in 1958 and the Libyan coup of 1969, it may have seemed that Rostow's "new elites" have finally come to the Arab world. The land-based elites have either lost, or are rapidly losing their grip on government policy and have been replaced by army officers. In at least one case, Egypt, they have been almost completely wiped off the political scene. Looking back, however, at the Arab "revolutionary" era, it now seems that one may do worse things than having

---

[29] See Azhari, *op. cit.*, pp. 110-2 and 120-1 and Himadeh, R.: *The Fiscal System of Lebanon*, Khayat, Beirut, 1961, pp. 74-5.

[30] Economist Intelligence Unit: *Syria, Lebanon & Cyprus*, No. 4, 1971, p. 6.

[31] In 1960, out of the 75 insurance companies operating in Lebanon 72 were foreign owned while foreign banks accounted for about 50% of all bank deposits. After the Intra crisis this percentage rose to 80%.

"country houses, servants, personal ornaments and temples" and that the Arab revolutionary governments may have at least as high a propensity to consume as the superseded landlords.

First, with military governments goes greater expenditure on armaments. There may not necessarily be more actual wars than with other kinds of government, but there are usually bigger and more expensively equipped armies. With the exception of Jordan, non-military Arab governments spend on defence smaller percentages of GNP and of the state budget than do the military ones, the lowest percentage of GNP being that of Lebanon.[32] In the year following the 1969 military coup in Libya, the *share* of defence expenditure in GNP rose by as much as 50%.[33] Since the 1967 war military expenditure in most of the nine countries rose more rapidly than national income, particularly in Egypt where it absorbed as much as 19.6% of GDP in 1970, this latter percentage being about two and a half times that of the U.S. (7.8%) and about 6 times that of India (3.4%).[34]

A simple calculation would reveal that to pay for the army the Iraqis, Egyptians and Syrians had to forgo an increase in investments of more than 50% in Iraq and of as much as 90% in Egypt and Syria.[35]

Secondly, for a number of well-known reasons, Arab bureaucracy has been famous for its inefficiency both before and after the revolutionary era. Poverty has always invited bribery, the reluctance to delegate authority bred apathy, while the age-long suspicion of corrupt governments encouraged the breaking of the law. Family and tribal relationships have been too entrenched to allow impersonalization and the deep-rooted charitable tradition of employing the inefficient simply to provide them with a means of livelihood, has been applied to government offices as much as to family firms. Arab revolutions only made things worse.

There is first the mere growth of an already inefficient mechanism

---

[32] See Table 20.

[33] International Institute for Strategic Studies: *The Military Balance*, 1971-2, pp. 60-1.

[34] *Ibid.* According to Egyptian sources, defence allocations in the 1970/1 budget were about $ 1300 million (*Al-Ahram*, 24.3.1971) a sum equal to 37% of total investments made during the first five-year plan. However, *actual* defence expenditure in 1971 was given by the International Institute for Strategic Studies as $ 1495 million. Official data tend to underestimate actual military expenditure and do not disclose the terms on which military aid is obtained.

[35] Compare Tables 17 and 20. In the 1972 state budget of Syria £S. 956 million was allocated to defence compared with total allocations in the development budget of 1594 million. (Economist Intelligence Unit: *Syria, Lebanon and Cyprus*, No. 1972, p. 3).

Table 20

Military Expenditure

	As % of Total State Budget (1965)	*As % of GNP*	
		1965	*Average 1966-70*
Egypt	22	9.1	13.8
Iraq	34	12.7	9.5
Syria	33	8.8	11.5
Jordan	47	12.0	15.1
Sudan	19	4.4	4.6
Libya	13	5.1	1.6
Kuwait	12	4.2	...
Lebanon	17	3.3	...
S. Arabia	19	8.6	9.2

(...) Not available.

Sources: International Institute for Strategic Studies: *The Military Balance*, 1970-1, pp. 110-1 and 1971-2, pp. 60-1 and Hurewitz, J.: *Middle East Politics: The Military Dimension*, Praeger, N.Y., 1969, pp. 106-7.

which accompanied the increasing role of governments in economic and social life. But new factors associated with revolutions tended to make Arab bureaucracies even more inefficient and wasteful. In revolutionary regimes political considerations gain supremacy over those of efficiency. The politically loyal is thus preferred to the able but politically passive, while highly-paid but fictitious jobs are created simply to accommodate a political figure removed from power but too dangerous to turn into an enemy. Even nationalization could be used against any economic reasoning merely to punish a political opponent or to create an appearance of ideological affinity with another Arab country, as happened in Iraq in 1964. New laws, taxes, exchange controls, import and export restrictions are incessantly introduced and are often too irrational to be observed, while new ministries and organizations are continuously established and then abolished. Of no little importance is also the fact that the new military rulers, being themselves younger than their predecessors and anxious to give the positions of power to those whom they can trust, tend to disregard the age of those appointed to high offices. S. Andreski perceptively points out the effect of this practice on the lower ranks of government bureaucracy:

> "Apart from reducing the incentives to effort, the small difference in age between the ranks aggravates the natural resentment against the authority which is usually less bitter if the boss is considerably older than the subordinates. It is not only that the prospect of seeing the old man off sweetens the pill of submission, but also the envy is diminished when the enjoyment of power and status is counter-balanced by the drawbacks of advancing years... This kind of equalisation permits the relationship of authority to become less tinged with paternal and filial feelings which become much more difficult if the difference in age is very small or inverse." [36]

Thirdly, loyalty or submission to the revolutionary governments is often more costly than that of the peasants to the landlord or of the industrial labourers to their employer. Whereas the landlord or capitalist could rely on a deeply ingrained feeling of servitude or fear, and sometimes even on genuine loyalty, the revolutionary governments, especially if unpopular, have to rely on a widespread network of political propaganda, police and intelligence activity or on the army. Thus it was probably less costly to move a peasant to vote for his landlord than to vote for a member of the revolutionary party. But the revolutionary governments are often more demanding than their predecessors. While previously it was sufficient to get enough votes to dominate a parliament, it seems necessary to a revolutionary Arab government to insist on obtaining some 99% of all votes. No one can deny that party politics leading to a mock parliament dominated by landlords is wasteful, but no smaller amount of resources are wasted on election campaigns under revolutionary governments in which there is only one candidate. The country's resources of foreign currencies, which are alleged to be meagre when there is a demand for imported books for university libraries, appear unlimited when it is a matter of gaining political supporters in other countries. While strikes are forbidden, working hours are lavishly spent on the reception of a friendly foreign politician or the demonstration against an unfriendly one.

Finally, there are the wastes resulting from political instability which has been particularly characteristic of Iraq and Syria. One writer counted no less than 265 "armed attacks" in Iraq between 1957 and 1965, armed attacks being defined as "acts of violence committed by or involving organized groups and weapons of any kind to protest or revolt against the regime, groups within the society including religious, ethnic, racial or interest groups". This is to be compared with only four such acts in

[36] *Op. cit.*, p. 155.

the previous eight years (1948-56).[37] For Syria, the same writer counts in the span of 25 years following her independence in 1946, about nine successful coups and four unsuccessful ones.

This instability of government in Iraq and Syria has considerably reduced the significance of economic planning,[38] discouraged private investment and caused a flight of capital, particularly from Syria.[39] It has also reduced the government's ability to mobilize savings, partly because of the inevitably higher costs of obtaining political support and partly because of the reluctance of new governments to raise tax rates.[40] No such instability characterized post-1952 politics in Egypt where the government was in fact more stable than in most underdeveloped countries during the same period. What Egypt did share with other Arab revolutionary governments, though again to a smaller degree, were the frequent changes in publicly declared policies concerning her political and economic relations with foreign powers and domestic private enterprise.

One result of all this was the failure of revolutionary Arab countries to achieve a significant increase in the rate of saving. Over the last two decades this rate has increased only slightly in Egypt, while in Syria and

---

[37] Al-Qazzaz, A.: Political Order, Stability and Officers, A Comparative Study of Iraq, Syria & Egypt, *Middle East Forum*, 1969, p. 34. In 1963 it was reported that one-half to three quarters of the people in Government posts involving any degree of real responsibility were new in their posts since the February coup. (See Jalal, F.: *The Role of Government in the Industrialization of Iraq*, Cass, London, 1972, p. 29).

[38] Dr F. Jalal gives the following example from Iraq: "One industrial project (sulphur extraction from natural gas) went through the whole process of pre-construction before 1958, and in June of that year the Development Board decided to contract the erection of the plant to an American firm at a total cost of I.D. 6,680,320 . . . then the revolution of July 1958 intervened and the firm was informed that the new government had decided to abrogate the Board's decision. The project was included in the Iraqi-Soviet Technical and Economic Cooperation Agreement of May 1959, to be studied and designed during 1959-62 and erected during 1962-4. After the revolution of February 1963 the project was withdrawn from the agreement and the process of reviewing and restudying started again. By January 1965 the contract for the erection of the project was signed with the original American firm at a cost of I.D. 7,485,900 for exactly the old project." (*Op. cit.*, p. 78).

[39] During the five years preceding 1964 capital flight from Syria was estimated at $ 200 million (Owen, *op. cit.*, p. 58).

[40] Thus between 1958 and 1964 the share of tax revenue in Iraq's national income rose from 12.3% to only 13.7% compared with an increase in the share of government current expenditure in national income from 27% to 34% during the same period. This tendency for tax revenue to fall as a percentage of government expenditure led the Iraqi government to the successive reduction of the proportion of oil revenue which according to the law should be directed to development, from the whole of oil revenue according to the 1950 law, to 75% of it in 1952 and to 50% in 1960.

Table 21

Average Annual Rates of Increase of Private and Public Consumption (%)

	Period	*Private Consumption*	*Public Consumption*
Iraq	1959-64	6.1	9.7
Syria	1956-64	4.5	13.0
Egypt	1959/60-64/5	6.5	14.2
Sudan	1955-64	5.8	10.8

Sources: U.N.: *Yearbook of National Accounts Statistics*, 1969; UNESOB: *Studies on Selected Development Problems*, 1967, p. 8 and 1969, p. 83 of the Arabic edition; U.A.R., Ministry of Planning: *Follow-Up and Evaluation Report on the First Five-Year Plan* (mimeo.), Feb. 1966, pp. 66-7.

the Sudan it showed a marked decline during the 1960's.[41] During 1960-67 the average rates of saving in the three countries were lower than that of underdeveloped countries taken as a whole (15%).[42] Even in Iraq the rate of saving remained fairly constant during the 1960's despite the rapid increase in oil revenue. Although the rapid increase in private consumption must certainly shoulder part of the blame, in all the four countries, Egypt, Syria, Iraq and the Sudan, public consumption was increasing much faster. Table 21 shows this for periods ending in the mid-1960's. For later years data are available only for Syria and Egypt and show that the same phenomenon continued through the late 1960's. In Egypt the share of public consumption in GNP rose more than three times as fast as private consumption during the period 1963-67 while in Syria the share of public consumption in GNP rose by 37% compared with a *decline* of 3% in the share of private consumption (1963-68).[43] In 1964 the Egyptian government, on realizing that foreign aid was not likely to be forthcoming at anything like previous rates, called for restraint. It is ironic that, although this had some effect on private consumption, it made little impression on the government itself. In the following three years, private consumption increased at an average annual rate of only 0.8% compared with 7.6% for public consumption.[44]

Furthermore, of the various components of public consumption, the items which grew most rapidly were not those which could be classified

[41] See Table 17.
[42] *The Pearson Report*, *op. cit.*, p. 31.
[43] U.N.: *Yearbook of National Accounts Statistics*, 1969.
[44] *Ibid.*

under development expenditures such as education or health, but rather the expenditures on ordinary administration and defence. Thus, between 1959/60 and 1965/6 the share in Egypt's GDP of government expenditure on defence and ordinary administration (excluding the administrative expenditures on health and education) almost doubled compared with an increase of about 25% in the share of education and health.[45] Similarly, about half of the increase in Syria's public consumption between 1956 and 1968 was due to defence expenditure. During the same period NDP from public administration grew at no less than 17.5% per annum compared with 4.2% for total NDP.[46] During the seven years following the 1958 revolutions of Iraq and the Sudan, government expenditure on development increased by 15% and 50% in the two countries respectively, compared with a 79% and a 62% increase in expenditure on ordinary administration and 153% and 273% on defence.[47] It is interesting to contrast these changes in the pattern of expenditure of the Iraqi government after the revolution with those before it. During the five years preceding 1958, government expenditure on defence, as well as on ordinary administration, did grow rapidly (74% and 68% respectively) but its expenditure on development increased much faster (360%).

3. *Oil Revenue and Foreign Aid*

Despite the big differences between the nine Arab countries with regard to the rate of saving, ranging from 1% in Jordan to 45% in Kuwait and Saudi Arabia, they are much closer to each other with regard to investment rates.[48] The reason is that, while the non-oil countries have been investing considerably more than their savings through the inflow of private foreign capital, as in Lebanon, or through foreign aid as in the other four countries, the oil countries have been investing much less than their savings. The last fact is particularly striking in the case of Iraq since her rate of saving, though high, is considerably below those of Saudi Arabia, Kuwait or Libya, and is certainly not beyond the absorptive capacity of the economy. Also remarkable is the decline in Iraq's rate of fixed capital formation from 24% in 1958 to 15% in 1965. Iraq's total investment in the non-oil sector, which showed a regular increase until

---

[45] See Hansen, B.: *Economic Development in Egypt*, Rand Corporation, 1969, p. 55.

[46] See Hansen, B.: *Economic Development in Syria*, Rand Corporation, 1970, p. VI and 11.

[47] Calculated from Hurewitz, J.: *Middle East Politics: The Military Dimension*, Praeger, N.Y., 1969, p. 160 & 169.

[48] See Table 17.

1957, has since then fluctuated with some tendency to decline.[49] Part of the explanation has to do with Iraq's failure to raise the rate of saving, but it is also connected with Iraq's performance in economic planning which will be discussed shortly.

More than half the very high rates of savings of Kuwait and Saudi Arabia is invested abroad, mainly in British Treasury Certificates, West European, American or Lebanese banks. This outflow of capital seems to have proceeded at a rate far exceeding the rate of aid flow into all the nine Arab countries combined. In the early 1960's the net outflow of financial resources from Kuwait and Saudi Arabia to the rest of the world exceeded $ 1 billion annually,[50] compared with an annual average of Sino-Soviet bloc commitments to all of the nine Arab countries of $ 175 million (1954-64) and an annual average of U.S.A. long-term aid to the same countries of $ 213 million (1945-1964). To put it another way, the flow of capital from Kuwait and Saudi Arabia alone in *one* year of the early 1960's amounted to more than one fourth of *total* U.S.A. long-term aid to the nine Arab countries *plus* the *total* economic aid commitments of the Sino-Soviet bloc to the same countries during the two decades following the war.[51]

While oil revenues finance the whole of investments in the oil countries as well as a good part of those of Lebanon, foreign aid finances the whole of Jordan's investments and a good part of those of Egypt, Syria and the Sudan. But whether financed by aid or by oil revenue, whatever is invested in both cases is not the result of any obvious sacrifice borne by the investor. This helps to explain why the government of an oil-rich country or of a country receiving vast amounts of foreign aid can enjoy a degree of stability which is not explicable in terms of its domestic economic or political performance. It also explains why wasteful expenditure is in the nature of both.

Professor Bauer remarks that:

> "Capital is much more likely to be productive when deployed by those groups and persons who accumulated it, because accumulation and effective deployment require much the same abilities, motivations and institutions." [52]

[49] UNESOB: *Studies on Selected Development Problems*, 1968, p. 2. During 1951-58 the average share of government capital expenditure in Iraq's national income was about 10%. In the following six years it rose to only 11.4%. (See Jalal, F., *op. cit.*, p. 72).

[50] UNESOB, *op. cit.*, 1967, p. 14.

[51] See Table 1.

[52] Bauer, P. T.: *Dissent on Development*, Weidenfeld & Nicolson, London, 1971, p. 103.

Although one should not carry this argument as far as to condemn any public investment of privately accumulated savings, it could rightly be used against excessive reliance on foreign aid as well as on oil revenues. It also rightly implies that only a government capable of realizing a high rate of saving is capable of channelling it into productive investment. Moreover, a government receiving vast amounts of either foreign aid or oil revenue is not likely to feel the urgent need for raising productivity, for increasing or diversifying exports or for tapping other sources of savings. Tax laws are likely to be lenient and tax evasion and income inequalities tolerated.

> "In societies severely afflicted by parasitism, the number of parasites seems to be governed by the amount of surplus (surplus being defined as the stock of goods in excess of the minimum subsistence requirements of the producers). Any augmentation of the surplus tends to increase the number of parasites and their consequent force in relation to the productive elements of society. An influx of funds from abroad usually stimulates the proliferation of superfluous administrative posts remunerated on a scale out of proportion to the economic possibilities of the receiving country, which whets the appetites and encourages the scramble for the spoils." [53]

An excessive reliance on either foreign aid or oil revenue also tends to generate economic and social imbalances simply because a country cannot import everything from abroad. Fine school buildings may indeed be provided with the most modern equipment by the use of aid or oil revenue, but no amount of such incomes will provide teachers who have the ability to converse in the country's own language, the same degree of knowledge of the country's history and culture or the same degree of loyalty as its nationals. An expansion of education by the use of foreign aid or oil income rather than as a response to the increasing need of the country's own industry or agriculture, is most likely to result either in a brain drain or in unemployment.[54]

Professor Bauer's statement that "if a country, or rather a people,

---

[53] Andreski, S.: *Parasitism and Subversion, the Case of Latin America*, Weidenfeld & Nicolson, London, 1966, pp. 257-8.

[54] See Bauer, *op. cit.*, pp. 105-6. Foreign aid may also obstruct effective economic integration among underdeveloped countries since it is hardly even distributed among them according to the potential harmonization and diversification of industrial development but is governed by the narrow economic and political relationship between the donor and the individual aid-receiving countries. For political as well as economic reasons the leading economies in the region tend to be favoured so that the differences between the level and potentialities of development of the various countries tend to grow. (See Wionczok, M. (ed.): *Economic Cooperation in Latin America, Africa and Asia*, MIT Press, Cambridge, Massachusetts, 1969, p. 17).

cannot readily develop without external gifts, it is unlikely to develop with them," [55] may seem to be disproved by Jordan's very rapid economic growth uptil 1967 which was entirely so financed. But we have already seen that private savings in Jordan would have been sufficient to finance half of her investment had it not been more than offset by the expenditure of the aid-receiving government.[56] Moreover, although Jordan's rate of growth was higher than most other Arab countries, her rate of investment was one of the lowest.[57] Foreign financed investment can therefore be only part of the explanation of her rapid growth. The rest is explained by Jordan's unusually low incremental capital-output ratio [58] which in its turn could, at least partly, be attributed to the extremely underdeveloped base, both in agriculture and manufacturing from which Jordan started twenty years ago. A very few obvious projects in agriculture or manufacturing could therefore make a marked contribution to total output. In agriculture, for example, the East Ghor Canal alone was estimated to have been responsible for about one fourth of the increase in the value added of all agricultural output between 1959/60 and 1965/66, while the establishment of only two firms, the petroleum refinery and a cement plant, represented an increase in value added in manufacturing of more than a third.[59]

Furthermore, just as one may argue that Jordan's reliance on foreign aid was due to her negative rate of savings, one may also argue exactly the opposite: that her low rate of savings was partly due to the large flow of aid, or that her excessively high expenditure on defence was made possible (if indeed it was not made necessary) by the flow of foreign aid. It could also be said that the increase in the flow of foreign aid to Egypt and Syria carries part of the blame for the very small increase in Egypt's rate of savings and its decline in Syria.

Most of the criticism directed to foreign aid centres either on the fact that it is not large enough, that it is economically or politically tied, or that its distribution among underdeveloped countries is governed by political and military considerations rather than by need. What seems to be the worst aspect of foreign aid, however, is the kind of political climate which it tends to foster in the aid-receiving country, particularly

---

[55] *Op. cit.*, p. 100.
[56] See Table 18.
[57] See Table 17.
[58] 1.5 during 1954-66 compared with about 3 for an average country at Jordan's level of income. (Mazur, *op. cit.*, p. 223.)
[59] *Ibid.*, pp. 258-61.

when it is as large as the aid received by Jordan or Egypt. In the 1962 National Charter of Egypt, one main aim of economic policy was stated to be "to raise both consumption and investment at the same time". This "difficult equation", as the problem was then called, had in fact been simply "solved" since 1956 by Nasser's success in securing vast amounts of aid. The real problem, however, was that the Egyptian government seems to have believed that to increase the country's ability to get more aid had no repercussions on its ability to raise the rate of saving so that if the former were no longer forthcoming all that had to be done was to rely on the latter. What happened was that by the time it became clear that the balance of payments had been too overburdened by the repayment and servicing of foreign loans to be ignored and that foreign aid was likely to be heavily reduced,[60] the government had already created a political and social climate in which it was almost impossible to fall back on the people's or the government's own ability to save. Privileged groups had already grown to such a degree of strength that their consumption patterns had to be allowed to continue; labour had already been accustomed to interpret "socialism" as higher wages for less work, and the country's development potential had come to be regarded as a matter of international politics, the secrets of which were known only to the president. Egypt had therefore no choice but to cut her rate of investment to bring it to a level with the country's low ability to save,[61] a course which was described by Hansen as "by far the most gloomy feature of the U.A.R. economy." [62] The high rate of growth which had been realized after 1956 could not therefore be maintained after 1963 when a decline set in and by 1966/7 it had fallen far below the rate of population growth.[63]

4. *Planning*

Just as each of the nine Arab countries has a flag and a national anthem, so it has a plan. Even Saudi Arabia, one year before Faisal emancipated the slaves, established the Higher Council for Planning

---

[60] The U.S. aid to Egypt, which consisted mainly of food, was reduced from its peak of $ 175 million in 1964 to $ 70 million in 1965 and $ 55 million in 1966. (Kanovsky, E.: *The Economic Impact of the Six-Day War*, Praeger, N.Y., 1970, p. 252).

[61] See Table 22.

[62] Hansen, B.: Planning and Economic Growth in the U.A.R. (1960-65), in Vatikiotis, P. (ed.): *Egypt since the Revolution*, Allen & Unwin, London, 1968, p. 37.

[63] Between 1962/3 and 1966/7 the annual rates of growth of GDP were 8.0, 6.4, 4.9, 4.5, and 0.7% for the respective years.

Table 22

Egypt: Gross Investment and Gross Domestic Savings as Percentages of GNP (1959/60-1968/69)

Year	*Gross Investment*	*Gross Domestic Savings*	*Year*	*Gross Investment*	*Gross Domestic Savings*
1959/60	12.5	12.8	1964/65	17.8	14.1
1960/61	15.5	14.4	1965/66	19.6	13.7
1961/62	16.6	10.9	1966/67	15.7	15.1
1962/63	17.8	11.6	1967/68	13.7	12.2
1963/64	19.7	12.5	1968/69	12.0	12.9

Source: Egyptian Ministry of Planning, *Follow-up and Evaluation Report on the First Five-Year Plan*, and *Annual Reports* of following years.

which three years later (1964) was substituted by the Central Planning Organization and a five-year plan was drawn-up in 1965.

One may wonder, however, whether the net benefits of introducing central planning in the Arab world have exceeded the salaries of the planners, the cost of planning and follow-up departments in the various ministries, the cost of the magnificent buildings occupied by planning ministries and institutes, of computers imported for their use, the generous payments made to foreign planning experts as well as the loss of whatever private productive investment may have taken place in the absence of planning but failed to materialize because of it.

All this may seem a small price to pay for ensuring the most rational allocation of resources. But to suppose that central planning necessarily leads to a more rational use of resources than the uncoordinated decisions of separate enterprises, whether privately or publicly owned, one must be making a large number of assumptions that have largely been unfulfilled.

First: One must be assuming that the country has at its disposal a sufficient number of qualified personnel as well as the necessary macro-economic and social data. An ECAFE study of planning in Asia and the Far East stated that "planning on the basis of inaccurate data may be worse than no planning at all, since such data may not only point to wrong solutions to problems but also create complacency and lead to serious bottlenecks and rigidities." [64] In most Arab countries both

[64] Quoted in Waterson, A.: *Development Planning, Lessons of Experience*, Johns Hopkins Press, Baltimore, 1969, p. 183.

planning expertise and the necessary statistics are seriously deficient. Yet, with their small numbers and working with such deficient data, and even with some data that certainly exists being withheld from them as belonging to the high secrets of the state, Arab planners often find themselves in the embarrassing situation of being asked to produce a "plan" in a few weeks.

When Syria started the formulation of her five-year plan 1960/61-64/5 the number of economists at her disposal did not exceed four or five [65] and when Lebanon's Ministry of Planning was first established it was composed of part-time employees. But even when the country is well equipped with the necessary planning personnel, as is the case with Egypt, planners, particularly the heads of planning agencies are usually also involved in several administrative and political tasks which are often taxing but more remunerative or promise greater rewards for their future careers.

While the lack of personnel can to some extent be met by calling upon foreign expertise, the lack of statistical data cannot. It is indeed difficult to take seriously the task of the Central Planning Organization of Saudi Arabia where the number of population is largely guesswork, with estimates of population made in the early 1960's ranging from 3.2 to over 6 million, to which was recently added another estimate made by the World Bank, of around 8 million.[66] More rewarding perhaps for the president of the organization is his other function as the principal political advisor to the king.

In 1961, two years before Libya's first five-year plan (1963-68) the IRBD mission reported that:

> "in agriculture, for example, no soil survey has yet been undertaken, records of land ownership are fragmentary and very little is known about the present pattern of land use ... Information about production in other sectors of the economy is even more scanty. There is no regular compilation of statistics of industrial production, and very little is known about movements of trade within the country ..." [67]

In neither Syria nor Lebanon has there ever been an agricultural census. The first population census of Syria was undertaken as late as 1960, but no population census has been undertaken in Lebanon since 1932 for

[65] Diab, M.: The First Five-Year Plan of Syria: An Appraisal, *Middle East Economic Papers*, 1960, p. 14.

[66] UNESOB: *Studies on Selected Development Problems*, 1968, p. 25, and Economist Intelligence Unit: Saudi Arabia & Jordan, No. 2, 1972, p. 4.

[67] IBRD: *Economic Development in Libya, op. cit.*, p. 89.

fear that the results may upset the balance maintained between the various religious sects. In his recent attempt at studying Syria's development prospects, Professor Hansen complained that while in view of the lack of data "the opinions and views of well-informed experienced people ... with inside information and a detailed, albeit unsystematic knowledge of the economy ... would have been extremely valuable ... the political state of the country has made it increasingly difficult to obtain even this sort of information. Syria is to-day a totalitarian state and the possibilities of communicating with knowledgeable Syrians are severely circumscribed ... Syriology is now a science almost comparable to Kremlinology." [68]

Thus in the first five-year plan of Syria there was no mention of sectoral or project capital-output ratios nor of the criterion which guided the authorities in their choice of projects.[69]

Secondly: the country must have administrative machinery the various organs of which have clearly delineated responsibilities, are allowed to take initiative and are flexible enough to meet unforseen circumstances which are bound to occur during the implementation of the plan. No Arab country is lucky enough to have such machinery with the result that investment projects which may appear coordinated in the plan are rarely so in their actual execution. Thus school or hospital buildings may stand empty because there are not enough students, teachers or doctors, the wages of labour may have been paid some months before the importation of the necessary machinery is even agreed upon, imported machinery and intermediate goods may reach the country before the factory is built or production may be interrupted because current expenditures are not authorized ... etc.

In Iraq, for example, because the construction of factories and the supply of raw materials are handled by different ministries, two sugar and tobacco factories, both publicly owned and constructed to use locally grown sugar beets and domestic tobacco, had to process imported raw sugar and imported tobacco because it was discovered, after the factories were built, that the domestic supply of sugar was unavailable and that domestic tobacco was not of the right quality.[70]

---

[68] *Economic Development of Syria* in Cooper & Alexander (eds.), *op. cit.*, p. 331.

[69] Diab, *op. cit.*, p. 23.

[70] Waterson, *op. cit.*, p. 311. For similar examples see, on Iraq, Badre, A.: *Economic Development of Iraq*, in Cooper & Alexander (eds.), *op. cit.*, p. 320; UNESOB: *Studies on Selected Development Problems*, 1969, p. 29 of the Arabic edition; and for Libya, Abu-Saud, M.: Petroleum Economics and Development in Libya, in *Pétrole et Dévelop-*

Thirdly: If a central plan is to be more than a mere expression of wishes the government must have a minimum degree of control over the basic conditions of its fulfilment. This control is obviously weaker the greater is the country's dependence in financing investment on uncertain foreign aid and the weaker its political position at home. The Egyptian confusion over the "second" five-year plan is a good example of the first difficulty while Iraq provides good examples of the second.

It was apparently the Egyptian government's uncertainty about the continuation of foreign aid that made it unable to publish the second development plan until well after the first had ended in June 1965, or even to decide whether it was going to be a seven, a five or a three-year plan. A three year "plan" was finally announced in December 1966 and was called an "accomplishment plan", meaning that, during these three years, only the projects which had already been started would be completed, a task which should have required no central plan at all. As late as 1971 it was announced that the third plan was being prepared but in fact there had never been a second. The Egyptian experience in planning of over ten years virtually consists, therefore, of the preparation of the first five-year plan (1959/60-64/5). During these ten years, however, both the Ministry and the Institute of Planning have expanded and moved to new modern buildings.

In contrast to Egypt, there is certainly no shortage of plans in Iraq. During a seven-year period (1951-58) Iraq had no less than four plans: 2 five-year and 2 six-year ones, and throughout her planning experience the average life span of a five-year plan was two years. Between 1964 and 1968 Iraq had 6 ministers of planning, 8 ministers of industry and transport, 7 ministers of public works and 6 ministers of land reform.[71] Successive Iraqi governments have therefore been powerless to bring the planned targets to fulfilment. Out of 39 major manufacturing projects included in the 1961-65 plan only four were completed by the beginning of 1965, while the feasibility of ten was still being studied. Over the whole period 1951-65, actual expenditures amounted only to 52.1% of total allocations.[72] Projects which had been included in one plan keep reappearing in the following ones. The industrial projects which appeared in the 1965-69 plan, for example, were almost the same as those included in the previous plan (1961-65). Nevertheless, the current cost of planning

---

pement Économique au Moyen-Orient, Publications de la Faculté du Droit et des Sciences Économiques de Grenoble, Editions Mouton, Paris, 1968, p. 93.

[71] See Badre, A.: *op. cit.*, p. 288 and UNESOB, *op. cit.*, p. 20.

[72] Jalal, F.: *op. cit.*, p. 65-74.

administration increased from I.D. 2.2 million in 1957 to 3.6 million in 1963.[73]

Despite their limited control over their country's political destiny and over the means of financing their plans, Arab governments, particularly the military ones, tend to set themselves targets which should seem over-ambitious even in the most favourable circumstances.

If private investors in Arab countries can be blamed for showing too much caution in their investment decisions and for concentrating on short-term profitability, Arab central planners are equally blameworthy for being too optimistic and for neglecting the short-term consequences of their plans in the hope of doubtful successes in the long-run. Just as over-cautiousness may deprive the country of some socially-desirable industries, over-ambitiousness may lead to the establishment of low-priority projects which were only a part of a big development programme that included more important but unrealized projects.

When Egypt embarked on her ambitious industrialization based on import-substitution, too much faith was put in the country's ability to export the new manufactured goods, as well as in the continuation of large sums of foreign aid. Factories were therefore built on a scale that could not be justified by the size of the home market alone. Too much was made of the foreign exchange that could be saved by replacing imports by home-made substitutes while little attention was given to the foreign exchange needed to import the necessary intermediate products and raw materials. The value of the latter often turned out to be higher than that of the former, partly because home production was now greater than the corresponding imports, and partly because of the inevitably lower efficiency in the use of raw materials. Thus, the share of raw materials and semi-finished goods in the total imports of 1965 was much higher than it was in 1952 and import substitution came to be "the substitution of imports by imports".[74] Total imports, far from decreasing as planned, increased at an annual average rate of 11.2% between 1960 and 1965.[75] When the export performance proved disappointing and foreign aid became insufficient for making good the shortages of raw materials and spare parts, unused capacity increased until 1965/66 when it was estimated that at least 25% of the productive capacity of national-

---

[73] *Ibid.*, p. 74.

[74] Mabro, R. and O'Brien, P.: Structural Changes in the Egyptian Economy, 1937-65, in Cook, M. (ed.): *Studies in the Economic History of the Middle East*, Oxford University Press, London, 1970, pp. 419-20 & 423-4.

[75] U.N.: *Survey of Economic Conditions in Africa - 1968*, N.Y., 1972, p. 74.

ized industries was idle.[76] In view of the high import content of investment,[77] the investment rate had to be reduced, as we have already seen.

Arab governments often recognize the ambitious character of their plans but they invariably seem to think that they will succeed where their predecessors have failed. Another explanation might lie in the political advantage of committing their countries to aims not all of which could be achieved, since this could continuously supply the government with excuses for taking unpopular measures or postponing popular ones. This may also explain why long-term plans are sometimes preferred, such as the ten-year plan of the Sudan (1960-70) or the seven-year plan of Jordan (1964-70), when the scarcity of data and the political and military uncertainties should have favoured shorter-term or even partial plans. It is sometimes argued that even though a country may not yet be ready for comprehensive planning it should nevertheless exercise it because it provides better education in planning for political leaders than partial planning. This argument is of doubtful significance in countries like Iraq or Syria where top planners are frequently changed. One may also argue that the educational benefit of any activity is most effective when the one being educated is convinced of the practical significance of his exercise. If this is true, then the successive failures in fulfilling the targets of comprehensive plans would make such planning of limited educational value. What is more likely to occur is an increase in apathy, at least among the lower ranks of planners. Indeed such factors have been reported as an explanation for the fact that most of the competent members of the Jordan Development Board left it after 1967.[78]

In many cases past economic performances, however recent, are rejected as a guide to possible developments in the future. Take, for example, Iraq's plan to increase public consumption at the same rate as GNP during 1965/66-69/70 when it had been increasing at a rate almost 50% higher during the previous 12 years; [79] or Syria's planned rate of growth of value added in agriculture in the 1966-70 plan of 7.5% annually compared with an annual average of 1.3% during 1956-67,[80] or Sudan's planned rate of growth of total output of 7.6% in her new

---

[76] IMF: *International Financial News Survey*, 9th Feb., 1968, p. 39 quoted in Musrey, *op. cit.*, p. 261.

[77] Nearly 50% during 1960-65 (Mabro & O'Brien, *op. cit.*, p. 423).

[78] Mazur, *op. cit.*, pp. 256-7.

[79] UNESOB, *op. cit.*, 1968, p. 5.

[80] Hansen, B.: *Economic Development in Syria*, Rand Corporation, 1970, p. 11.

plan (1970/1-74/5) [81] compared with a rate of growth of less than 4% during 1960-67.

Although the planned rate of growth of 5% in Sudan's earlier ten-year plan (1960-70) appears more modest, it should also be regarded as too ambitious considering the planned rate of increase in imports of only 2% and the implied rate of growth of industry, building and public utilities of 13.4% per annum. This last rate seems all the more unrealistic if one considers that while public investment was planned to represent 66% of total investment, public investment in industry was planned to contribute only 33% of total investments in this sector. This means that the "realization of the most ambitious target of the plan is largely left to the private sector ... (and) that realization of the plan depends on forces which can be influenced and channelled by government action to a very limited extent only." [82]

Defective implementation of a plan may be due neither to excessive reliance on unreliable foreign aid, nor to political instability, nor to the over-ambitiousness of targets but simply to the fact that the declared targets, or indeed the whole plan, was never intended to be more than window-dressing. This is particularly true of Lebanese planning. In the Lebanon it is customary to employ, at great cost, foreign experts whose reports are often sound but rarely used. Very few of the recommendations made ten years ago by the IFRED mission, for example, have been adopted other than those concerning the creation of new administrative departments and organizations. This was in spite of the fact the IFRED mission had been realistic enough to recognize the limitations in the role of government in Lebanon not going beyond advising the government of the means by which it could direct the activities of the private sector and concentrate its own efforts on developing the country's infrastructure.[83] Similar reasons may also have been behind the very low percentages of planned development expenditure which were actually achieved by Kuwait and Libya,[84] and behind the deviation in the pattern of actual

[81] *Middle East International*, A Special Supplement on the Sudan, May, 1972, p. 9,

[82] Gusten, R.: *Problems of Economic Growth & Planning: The Sudan Example*. Springer-Verlag, Berlin, 1966, pp. 30-35.

[83] See Azhari, *op. cit.*, pp. 71-2 and 89; U.N.: 1970 *Report on the World Social Situation*, p. 77, and Corm, G.: *Politique Économique et Planification au Liban*, 1953-63, Librairie de Medicis, Paris, (1965?).

[84] In Kuwait, actual development expenditure in the public sector during the first four years of the five-year plan (1967/8-71/2) amounted to about 49% of the proposed five-year total. In Libya the corresponding ratios were 58.7% and 66.8% for the first and second years of the 1963-68 plan, respectively. (See: Economist Intelligence Unit: *The Arabian Peninsula*, Annual Supplement, 1971, p. 8, and Farley: *Development Planning in Libya*, Praeger, N.Y., 1971, p. 228).

investment expenditure in Iraq from that of planned expenditure, so that the share of buildings in the former came to be one third higher than in the latter, at the expense of both agriculture and industry (see Table 23).

Table 23

Iraq: Deviation of the Actual Pattern of Expenditure from Planned Composition of Investment (1951-65)

	1951-58		1959-65	
	Planned	*Actual*	*Planned*	*Actual*
Agriculture	34.3	32.2	18.7	13.5
Industry	14.8	12.6	22.5	17.1
Communication	26.0	20.3	25.5	24.9
Buildings	24.9	34.9	33.3	44.5
Total	100.0	100.0	100.0	100.0

Source: Jalal, F.: *The Role of Government in the Industrialization of Iraq*, Cass, London, 1972, p. 68.

Finally, to suppose that the introduction of central planning necessarily leads to a more rational use of resources one has to assume, above all, that the paramount *objectives* of those who determine the broad plan targets and the means for their implementation, are economically superior to those of private investors or managers of public enterprises. Although it is often taken for granted that this is the case, it is far from obvious in the case of top-policy makers in the Arab world who almost always seem ready to sacrifice economic development if it comes in conflict either with their gaining a political advantage or with the economic interests of a politically influential group. Nor is it obvious that even the planned allocation of investments among the various sectors has been governed by criteria that are socially superior to the pursuit of purely private interests.

After the 1958 revolution in Iraq, the government declared the aim of its first plan (1959-62) as "to change radically the direction of the plan of the previous regime ... in a manner which can serve the interests of the Iraqi people." In this plan, however, first priority was given to public buildings and housing (48.7% of total allocations).[85] In the 1960-65 plan out of I.D. 27 million allotted to housing, 10 million were for army officers' houses in Baghdad and the remaining 17 million were allotted

[85] Jalal, *op. cit.*, pp. 38-9.

to other cities, with nothing assigned to rural housing. Again, in the 1961-65 Plan I.D. 11 million were allotted to build a new civil airport in Baghdad, 9 million for radio and television stations, 33 million for new buildings for Baghdad University, 5 million for Baghdad roads, 6.2 million for providing the post and telephone department with more modern equipment and 2.5 million for prisons compared, for example, with only half a million for agricultural cooperatives. A new building for the Ministry of Planning itself was allotted I.D. 1.8 million.[86] Only political objectives can explain such a pattern of expenditure. In Egypt, such objectives must explain the distribution of profits and bonuses whether the planned targets are fulfilled or not, or the refusal to recognize the right of a manager to dismiss a negligent labourer or the promotion of a minister who has obviously been responsible for a big waste of investments. It is also largely by political factors that one can explain why, in many Arab plans, a greater proportion of investment is allocated to services, housing and public utilities than to agriculture or industry,[87] and why in some of them, as in Egypt's first five-year plan, a good part of industrial investments was directed to such industries as those producing air-conditioners, refrigerators and private motor cars. The Egyptian steel industry as well as the Iraqi agricultural machinery project, both largely financed by foreign aid, may have been politically attractive but in both cases the country possesses neither the required raw materials, nor the market that could absorb the products, nor any special advantage in producing them.[88]

5. *Education*

Political factors have also been responsible for several features of the development of the Arab educational system. The problem here is not that Arab governments have been spending too little,[89] but rather that

[86] Hasan, S.: *Studies in the Iraqi Economy* (Arabic), Dar-El-Taliâa, Beirut, 1966, pp. 258-68.

[87] The planned share in total investments of dwellings, public utilities, transport and other services were: 40.3% in Egypt (1960-65), 53.6% in Iraq (1959-64), 57.4% in Jordan (1964-70) and 51.5% in Syria (1960-65). In Sudan's ten-year plan "social administration" was allotted 26.5% of total investment compared with 21% for agriculture and 18.9% for industry, mining and public utilities.

[88] See on the Egyptian steel industry, Hansen, B.: *Economic Development in Egypt*, The Rand Corporation, 1969, pp. 19-20 and on Iraq's production of agricultural machinery, Jalal, *op. cit.*, p. 57.

[89] In 1966-67 public expenditure on education as a percentage of total government expenditure ranged between 9.5% in Kuwait to 23.9% in Syria, and as a percentage of GNP from 2.7% in Lebanon to 5.9% in Iraq. (UNESCO: *Statistical Yearbook*, 1970.)

the distribution of their expenditure among the various types of education has been faulty, and that its expansion has been at the expense of the quality of learning.

Accepting a class bias against manual labour, Arab governments have allowed general secondary education to outgrow technical and vocational training. But on facing an increasing number of students who, having finished their secondary education, demanded places in the university, the governments again yielded to the pressure by expanding university education, particularly the less costly faculties of arts and humanities, out of all proportion with the employment opportunities for university graduates. Faced with another political problem resulting from the unemployment of university graduates, Arab governments have again yielded to the pressure by overburdening the state budget with the cost of supporting university graduates irrespective of their actual contribution to production. Meanwhile illiteracy rates were allowed to remain surprisingly high.

In the early 1960's illiteracy rates for the age group 15-24 years was not lower than 55%, except in Lebanon (10.2%) and Jordan (38.0%) and no less than 95% in Saudi Arabia.[90] If such a high rate is understandable for countries like Saudi Arabia, where university education had started only a few years before, or like the Sudan, where the first secondary school in the southern provinces was not opened until 1948, it is much more difficult to understand why Egypt, which had introduced modern university education more than half a century before, should still have a 75% illiteracy rate among the same age group in 1960. Since 1960, the countries which had the highest illiteracy rates witnessed a rapid increase in their primary-school enrolment. This is not true of Egypt, however, where the rate was not much higher than the rate of population growth.[91] Thus, as late as 1967, Egypt still had an illiteracy rate of 75% for persons above 10 years old.[92]

The mere lack of financial resources is no more acceptable as an excuse for allowing such high illiteracy rates to persist than as an excuse for other deficiencies. According to an estimate made for Egypt by

[90] UNESOB: *Studies on Selected Development Problems*, 1970, pp. 79-84.

[91] See Table 24.

[92] *Al-Ahram*, 26.2.1971. In 1955 the Egyptian government announced a program by which all children of the age group 6-12 would find a place in school by 1964. By 1965 the enrolment ratio was still only 40%. The program was replaced by another aiming at absorbing all the 6-year-old by 1969. By 1971 this had not yet been achieved. (See Issawi, Charles: *Egypt in Revolution*, London, 1963, pp. 91-2 and Abdallah, Ismail, Basic Principles in the Planning of Education, *Al-Taliaa*, Feb. 1971, p. 82).

Table 24

Average Annual Rates of Growth of School Enrolment
(%)

Country	*Period*	*Primary*	*Secondary*
Lebanon	1958-66	7	13
Jordan	1958-66	5	8
Syria	1961-68	7	13
Libya	1960-67	10	16
Iraq	1957-66	10	17
Kuwait	1956-65	14	19
Egypt	1960-67	4	13
Sudan	1960-67	7	11
Saudi Arabia	1958-67	11	19

Source: UNESOB: *La Croissance Économique, op. cit.*, p. 47.

Table 25

School Enrolment (1965)

	School Enrolment Ratios		*Students Enrolled in Secondary Technical Schools as % of all Students*
Country	*Primary* (%) [a]	*Secondary* (%) [b]	
Lebanon	52	33	0.3
Jordan	57	49	0.8
Syria	45	38	0.9
Libya	46	28	...
Iraq	41	29	0.6
Kuwait	51	80	1.2
Egypt	40	21	...
Sudan	13	7	...
Saudi Arabia	15	5	0.9

[a] Number of students enrolled in primary schools as a percentage of estimated population 5-14 years old.
[b] Number of students enrolled in all secondary schools (general, vocational, teacher-training) as percentage of estimated population 15-19 years old.
(...) Not available.

Source: UNESOB: *Studies on Selected Development Problems*, 1970, pp. 79-84.

UNESCO, teaching one person to read and write does not, or at least should not cost more than £E. 2.4 including his share in the cost of administration, inspection, propaganda, teachers and teaching equipment.[93] The total cost of teaching about 16 million illiterate Egyptians above the age of 10 to read and write would therefore be no more than £E. 40 million, a sum certainly within the reach of the Egyptian administration.

Enrolment ratios in primary schools (i.e. the number of students as a proportion of the number of population at primary-school age) had nowhere reached 60% in 1965 and, except for Kuwait, is considerably lower for secondary schools.[94] These ratios, however low, can still be misleading since they do not allow for the large percentages of dropouts nor for the relapse into illiteracy, particularly in rural areas, because of the lack of reading materials and other educational facilities. A UNESCO mission to Iraq, for example, found that, for the period 1949-63, only about 65% of those who entered primary school reached the sixth grade, 29% reached the third secondary, 19% reached the fifth secondary and only 12% passed their secondary school certificate. Among the reasons given for the large percentage of dropouts were the dependence of parents on their children's assistance as farm hands, the inaccessibility of some schools, the traditional seclusion of older girls and the financial burden of schooling on parents.[95]

Enrolment in technical schools has been growing much more slowly than in secondary schools providing a general education. For example, compared with a 13% annual rate of growth of enrolment in all secondary schools in Syria and Lebanon, enrolment in technical schools was growing at only 3% in Lebanon (1958-66) and declining by 3.4% annually in Syria (1961-68).[96] Similarly, an absolute decline in enrolment in technical schools occurred in Iraq and their share in all secondary school students declined from 21% in 1957 to 4% in 1967.[97] Technical secondary education therefore still absorbs a very low proportion of all students, the highest, that of Kuwait, being 1.2% compared with 8.3% in France and 31.4% in U.S.A.[98]

Arab countries can indeed boast of enrolment ratios in higher educa-

[93] This estimate was made on the assumption that out of a class of 40 students, 30 would successfully finish the course. (UNESCO: *The Organization and Financing of Literacy Campaigns in Arab Countries*, (Arabic), Serse El-Layyan, Egypt, 1965, p. 127).

[94] See Table 25.

[95] U.N.: *1970 Report on the World Social Situation*, p. 74.

[96] UNESOB: *La Croissance Économique*, *op. cit.*, p. 54.

[97] *Ibid.*, pp. 151-3.

[98] See Table 25. According to the same source (p. 158) technical secondary education in Iraq was allotted 2.1% of total public expenditure on education in 1966, compared with 17.2% for secondary general education and 12.0% for higher education.

tion comparable to those of some advanced countries. Jordan, for example, has the same ratio of higher-education students to total population as have France and Sweden (11 per thousand) while Syria, Lebanon and Egypt have about the same ratio as Western Germany and Britain (5 to 6 per thousand). In 1966, between 60 and 80% of all students in Arab universities were studying arts, social sciences and humanities, and not more than a third, except in Egypt and Iraq, were studying applied sciences and sciences proper. Among the latter, only a small fraction was studying agriculture.[99]

A useful distinction is that between consumption education and investment education.

"Teaching an African cook to read may increase his enjoyment of life but will not necessarily make him a better cook." [100]

Table 26

Enrolment in Higher Education (1966)

Country	*Higher-Education National Students Per 1000 of Population*	*Percentages of Higher Education Students Learning:*	
		Law, Social Sciences & Humanities	*Other*
Lebanon	6	83	17
Jordan	11	85	15
Syria	6	71	29
Libya	2	73	27
Iraq	3	54	46
Kuwait	3	79	21
Egypt	5	52	48
Sudan	1	68	32
Saudi Arabia	1	71	29

Sources: UNESCO: *Statistical Yearbook*, 1969 and UNESOB: *Studies in Selected Development Studies*, 1970, pp. 79-84.

[99] See Table 26. Of all students in higher education, those studying agriculture did not constitute more than 1.6% in Syria (1967), 1.9% in Lebanon (1969), 4.1% in Saudi Arabia (1966) and 4.9% in Jordan (1966). The same bias is also observed in secondary technical schools where the ratio is two students at agricultural schools for every ten at industrial ones (UNESOB: *La Croissance Économique*, *op. cit.*, p. 56 and El-Koussy, A. A.: Education in the Arab States of the Middle East, in Adams, M. (ed.): *The Middle East, A Handbook*, Anthony Blond, London, 1971, p. 510).

[100] Lewis, A.: Education and Economic Development, in *Social and Economic Studies*, Vol. X, no. 2, June 1961, p. 113.

By the same token educating thousands of students every year in law, commerce or the humanities only to appoint them as government clerks is merely consumption education, although it is more doubtful, in this case, that their enjoyment of life is thereby increased considering the disappointment they continuously feel. Their productive capacity may indeed be lower, because of their discontent, than if the same job was done by others who are far less educated. In most Arab countries even a large part of postgraduate education could be so regarded considering that even university professors are often engaged in routine work which indeed reduces their capacity for teaching and research. But what is probably the worst example of wasted education is the recruitment of highly qualified persons in political activities which could be better done by others, or better still, not done at all.

While this distribution of university students has resulted in an oversupply of graduates of faculties of law, commerce and the arts, the slow increase of enrolment in technical education has created shortages in intermediate technicians such as foremen, laboratory assistants, nurses ... etc. In some countries, particularly Syria and Lebanon, even the supply of engineers and natural scientists seems to have exceeded the demand for them.[101] What is certain is that the conditions of work offered to them are becoming increasingly inadequate compared with what they are offered abroad. Between 1962 and 1967 more than 5000 professional and technical workers emigrated from five Arab countries to U.S.A. and Canada alone of whom 50% were Egyptians.[102] Of all scientists and engineers emigrating from Egypt about 70% have Ph.D. and 17.5% have Master's degrees.[103] During the same period Jordan lost to the U.S.A. and Canada about one third of her 1961 stock of natural scientists.[104]

But by far the grimmest feature of Arab education is the quality of what is taught. This again is not merely a quantitative matter of the little amount of knowledge acquired in Arab schools whereby the student may leave the primary school hardly able to read and write, nor of the low teacher-student ratios [105] nor of the poor equipment of schools and univer-

---

[101] See Table 27.

[102] See Table 28.

[103] *Al-Ahram*, 2.1.1970.

[104] Godfrey, E.: The Brain Drain from Low-Income Countries, *Journal of Development Studies*, April, 1970, p. 238.

[105] According to official statistics, between 1953/4 and 1965/6 the number of students for every teacher increased from 30 to 40 in primary schools, from 12 to 19 in general secondary schools and from 6 to 13 in technical secondary schools. Another source

Table 27

Ratio of the Annual Number of Emigrants to France, U.S.A. and Canada to the Annual Number of Graduates From the Related Field of Study by Country of Last Permanent Residence (1962-66)

	Engineers	*Natural Scientists*	*Physicians*	*Nurses*	*Social Scientists*
	F+U.S.+C	F+U.S.+C	F+U.S.+C	U.S.+C	U.S.
Iraq	9.2	—	4.9	—	0.1
Jordan	—	∞	∞	21.8	∞
Lebanon	35.5	10.5	24.9	—	0.5
Syria	56.5	11.7	9.3	—	0.8
Egypt	1.9	4.6	3.7	1.1	0.06

(—) Not available.
(∞) Indicates that there were emigrants in the category concerned but no new graduates.

Source: as for table 28, pp. 190-1.

Table 28

Immigrants Admitted into U.S.A. and Canada by Country of Origin

Country	*Total Immigrants (1962-67)*	*Professional and Technical Workers (1962-67)*	*Engineers*	*Natural Scientists*	*Physicians*	*Professional Nurses*
			1962-1966			
Egypt	15901	2403	172	76	165	21
Lebanon	6674	956	155	56	91	55
Syria	2071 [a]	384 [a]	71	22	15	8
Iraq	3382 [b]	657	99	48	24	8 [c]
Jordan	6302 [b]	694	54 [c]	38	14	16

[a] For immigrants into U.S.: 1963-66.
[b] For immigrants into Canada: 1964-66.
[c] Admitted into U.S. only.

Source: Henderson, G.: *The Emigration of Highly-Skilled Manpower from the Developing Countries*, United Nations Institute for Training and Research, (mimeo.), N.Y., 1970, pp. 170-2.

---

mentions a decline in the staff-student ratio in the arts colleges in Egyptian universities from 1 : 7 in 1930 to 1 : 60 in 1962. (U.A.R. Central Agency for General Mobilization and Statistics: *Population growth and its Challenges to Development*, 'Arabic', Cairo, 1966, p. 192; Vatikiotis, P.: *The Modern History of Egypt*, Weidenfeld & Nicholson, London, 1969, p. 425. See also Awad, L.: *The University and the New Society*, 'Arabic', Al-Dar Al-Kawmeya, Cairo, 1965? and Qubain, F.: *Education and Science in the Arab World*, Johns Hopkins Press, Baltimore, 1966).

sities in educational means. More important is that much of what is taught is irrelevant or outdated, that the existing system of education discourages independent thinking, obliterates the country's history in the name of revolution, ignores national characteristics in the name of progress and deprives the rural population of their most promising members in favour of the city.

One prominent Egyptian educationalist, commenting on the quality of the Egyptian educational system, wrote:

> "Students still absent themselves from school a month or six weeks before final examination in order to cram. Examination questions test facts and informational material rather than thinking, and textbooks are over-condensed. To make matters worse, teachers compress the texts into abridged notes, which in turn the students abridge further into nut-shell facts to be reproduced in the examinations. Even on the university level, instructors often lean heavily on one text-book with no collateral readings, and in many cases hold their students responsible only for their mimeographed or private notes ... Even those schools which have libraries with a few books and periodicals do not offer any facilities to enable either teachers or students to profit by them. In many cases, these books and periodicals are locked up most of the time and are beyond the reach of those who desire to read ... For over a century, up to a decade or two ago, Egypt boasted of the fact that its educated men and women, even though comprising a minor proportion of the population, were well conversant with foreign languages, notably English and French. Following World War II, however, enthusiasm for teaching these languages became noticeably lukewarm. Students were allowed to receive their secondary certificate and join the universities with a low passing grade and lately even with failures in those languages... Formerly, those who taught English and French ... were English and French-speaking men and women. Now they are all Egyptians, or residents from other countries. Only a minute fraction of these are competent to teach these languages..." [106]

Of the effect of the revolution on Egyptian education, Dr Louis Awad gives the following examples. In the history book taught to 12-year old Egyptian students, out of 70 pages covering Egypt's history from the year 1517 to the present, one third is dedicated to the 15 years following the 1952 revolution, the remaining two thirds being dedicated to the history of about 435 years. The same student is told that one of three reasons responsible for Mohamed Ali's failure to establish "a great state" is that he was not of Arab origin and did not speak Arabic. He is not told however who sat on Egypt's throne between 1919 and 1936. The name of

---

[106] Boktor, A.: *The Development and Expansion of Education in the U.A.R.*, American University in Cairo Press, Cairo, 1963, pp. 163-8.

the following king, Farouk, is mentioned only because of his connection with the 1952 revolution.[107]

The kind of education which is provided for the inhabitants of Arab villages is not designed in a way that could help the villagers themselves, but merely prepares their children for employment in the towns. A study of education in rural Iraq was conducted in a village lying in one of Iraq's most fertile rice-producing areas near the city of Amara, given the fictitious name of "Umm Al-Nahr" by the author in order to protect confidences. The school which the author describes in the following quotation serves this village as well as some thirty-five or forty other villages in the district:

> "Although rural school teachers are somewhat below the standard of town and city teachers, the poor showing of this school and others like it is not primarily dependent upon teaching standards or upon a lack of intelligence among the students, the reasons so often cited in Iraq. This poor record is rather a function of the unsuitability of the school curriculum for the students and the consequent lack of village association with the school. The school teaches, in effect, an alien curriculum suitable for Baghdad, for which it was designed.
>
> I call the curriculum alien since it has no real relevance or meaning to the village children. Their world is limited to the immediate neighbourhood of the village, still closer to the world of Ur and Babylon than it is to our modern world. Yet the school attempts to bridge this vast gap and to prepare the students for life in this other world, which does not as yet exist for them. The school, by teaching the three R's, geography, civics, hygiene, physical education, and even English, attempts to equip the students for a world which is meaningless. Hygiene classes, for instance, teach the village boy that, if he brushes his teeth, gets exercise, a balanced diet and keeps clean, etc., he will be healthy. This sort of lesson makes a great deal of sense for a boy who lives in New York or Iowa or even Baghdad, but bears no relationship to life in Umm al-Nahr, where animal dung is used for fuel, where barefoot peasants walk through fields infested with hookworm, and where the only drinking water available is almost certain to be contaminated.
>
> If, despite all the difficulties facing the village boy, he attains his certificate and bridges the gap between Umm al-Nahr and the modern world, his value to the village is less than it would have been had he remained illiterate. By becoming literate, he has become superior to his neighbours in the village who have been unable to bridge the gap. He then goes to the city to 'make his fortune' as a minor government worker, a labourer, a clerk or employee in some other low-level position." [108]

---

[107] *Al-Ahram*, 19.3.1971.

[108] Quint, M.: The Idea of Progress in an Iraqi Village, in: Nolte, R. (ed.): *The Modern Middle East*, Atheron Press, N.Y., 1963, pp. 113-114.

A depressing example of the thoughtless attempt at "modernizing" Arab education at the expense of national characteristics is provided by the Egyptian revolution's "reform" of Al-Azhar, as a result of which one of the oldest universities in the world has been reduced to a miserable replica of the existing state universities. Rather than trying to rid it of its medieval scholasticism while preserving its age-old functions of training theologians and specialists in Islamic law for the whole of the Muslim world, the government hastily announced a bill of reform which became law in July 1961 virtually amounting to its "nationalization". The Azhar Shaykh was described by the president as "a stooge of reaction, feudalism and capitalism" and the reform was presented as necessary if Al-Azhar is "to adapt itself to contemporary times", if the Africans trained at Al-Azhar could find jobs when they returned home and if its graduates were to become "capable of production ... and able to participate in ... progress." [109]

Al-Azhar thus became the fifth Egyptian state university and to the old faculties teaching religious subjects and Arabic languages were added new faculties for business administration, agriculture, engineering and medicine, instruction in the last two being in English. "In vain went the Shaykh's attempts to point out that Azharis could not possibly study *tafsir* and medicine side by side, the work load being too great." [110] On the resignation of some of Al-Azhar Shaykhs' in protest the government appointed Western educated "Shaykhs" in their place so that, by 1966, all the deans of Al-Azhar university were holding Ph.D. degrees. The Imams began to be trained to teach socialism to the masses. The old tradition of Al-Azhar according to which the students were allowed freely to discuss what they hear from their Shaykhs, to chose their teachers as well as the time of examination, gave way to the more

[109] Crecelius, D.: Al-Azhar in the Revolution, *Middle East Journal*, Winter, 1966, pp. 39-42.

[110] *Ibid.* According to this source, the government's reform of Al-Azhar was declared in such haste that forces which might have opposed it were never given time to defend Al-Azhar. A committee was formed to discuss the proposed reforms including government as well as Shaykhs' representatives. "Two bills were submitted for consideration, one supposedly representing the government's and one the Shaykh's. Both, however, seem to have been prepared by the government since the unpublished minutes clearly reveal that the Azharis did not know what was in their version. They asked for adjournment in order to study its contents ... Handicapped by a lack of knowledge concerning parliamentary procedure they were constantly silenced on points of order ..." (*ibid.*, p. 38). See also: Kraemer, J.: Tradition and Reform at Al-Azhar University, in Rivlin, B. & Szyliowicz, J. (eds.): *The Contemporary Middle East, Tradition and Innovation*, Rand House, N.Y., 1965, pp. 338-43. For a sympathetic view of the reform see Boktor, *op. cit.*, p. 195.

"modern" system of regular examinations and of textbooks being forced on the students. Meanwhile the high prestige enjoyed by Al-Azhar Shaykhs in the Muslim world continued to be used by the government in support of its international and domestic policies.

6. *Arab Nationalism*

A most powerful force in the economic development of the now-advanced countries, "at least as important as the profit motive", was, according to Rostow, the force of reactive nationalism. "Men holding effective authority or influence have been willing to uproot traditional societies not, primarily, to make money but because the traditional society failed, or threatened to fail—to protect them from humiliation by foreigners." [111] National reaction to past humiliation or to a serious threat of foreign intervention was, according to Rostow "the great engine of change" in Germany, Russia, Japan and China as well as in England.[112]

Many of the psychological traits which are generally recognized to be generated or enforced by war could also be generated by a strong nationalist movement against an existing foreign occupation or the danger of a foreign threat. Among these are a strong sense of loyalty to the homeland and of social solidarity, an unusual readiness to accept new sacrifices and a strong desire to prove one's nation to be equal, or superior, to the foreigner. Just as these qualities may be conducive to victory in war they also can, if they last long enough, be favourable to econonomic development through their positive effects on the amount of effort and initiative as well as savings.[113]

In the Arab world such a wave of enthusiasm and national pride seems to have existed during the second half of the 1950's. This was first generated by Nasser's strong opposition to the treaty known as the Baghdad Pact in 1955 which, of all Arab countries, only Iraq dared to sign; by his arms deal with Czechoslovakia in September of the same year, but mainly by Nasser's nationalization of the Suez Canal in 1956 and shortly after by his proud rejection of the Eisenhower Doctrine (1957-8), and again when Egypt triumphantly united with Syria in

[111] *The Stages of Economic Growth, op. cit.*, pp. 26-7.

[112] *Ibid.*, pp. 27-35.

[113] Arthur Lewis notes the favourable effect which such a general mood of enthusiasm can have on literacy campaigns, especially among adults, indeed its very necessity for the success of such campaigns, thus "the Danish folk movement or the Russian literacy campaigns or any other adult education movement has been successful in so far as it has stirred the imaginations of the people and created a mass desire to learn." (*Education and Economic Development, op. cit.*, pp. 121-2)

February 1958. It was at that time that Nasser had possessed a degree of power and popularity never achieved before or since, when he was hailed not only in the Arab world but all over the third world as a symbol of their revolt against "the humiliation by foreigners." A civil war followed in Lebanon in April-May 1958 which was essentially a battle between pan-Arabist groups and the separatists among the Lebanese who favoured the continuation of an independent Lebanon with closer ties with the Western Powers. Nationalist feelings were only intensified by the landing of U.S. marines in Lebanon, of British paratroops in Amman and again by the Iraqi revolution in July. In the following month King Saud reluctantly yielded to the pressure of influential Saudis and appointed Prince Faisal to the presidency of the Council of Ministers with unlimited power to govern the country, and a number of reforms were hurriedly introduced.

In the words of Professor Vatikiotis, as a result of Nasser's political victories of this period:

> "his Arab detractors or rivals, 'Nuri-al-Said of Iraq, King Saud of Arabia, King Idris of Libya and others' were cowed, the Lebanese were terrified, the British and French humiliated and the Americans awed by their belief that the Arab-world had surely found its Bismarck." [114]

To many people in the West, the Arab nationalist movement of the 1950's may have appeared too aggressive and possibly naive, and the slogan of "positive neutrality" which was raised at the time, as little more than a myth. To the Arabs, however, these were glorious years and, looking back at them one can hardly avoid noting that the political climate which prevailed during them, had it lasted, could have been most favourable to economic development. Nor can one avoid noting that these were also Egypt's best years of the whole of the past two decades not only in economic performance but even in the vitality of cultural life. In fact, had the Arab nationalist movement of that period borne its full economic fruits, Rostow would most probably have found in it new evidence of the truth of his theory. Having failed, however, Rostow, in his new book, did not hesitate to condemn it.[115]

For about a decade following the eventful year of 1958 neither Israel nor the Western Powers ventured seriously to provoke the Arabs. Whether or not this was a direct result of the failure of the opposite policy, it was certainly a major cause of the decline of the Arab nationalist

---

[114] Vatikiotis, P.: *Conflict in the Middle East*, Allen & Unwin, London, 1971, p. 132,
[115] *Politics and the Stages of Growth*, Cambridge University Press, Cambridge, 1971. pp. 279-82.

movement. While deprived of the target of an obvious Western threat, no substitute seemed powerful enough to arouse dormant nationalists. When the threat of an Israeli attack rose again in May 1967 nationalist feelings were suddenly aroused and Nasser's popularity quickly soared, but the whole crisis did not last for more than a few weeks.

Neither the ideal of socialism, nor of economic independence, nor of a unified Arab state seemed able to do the job. Nationalization did not make much sense to a country relying on trade or tourism, like Lebanon, or with a small industrial base like most of the rest. Soon after the Suez affair the only significant foreign private investment in Arab countries, other than Lebanon, was that of the oil companies, but neither Nasser nor any other Arab leader made a public issue of their nationalization. It seemed neither economically rewarding nor, in the light of the attitude of the governments of the oil countries, politically feasible. In the aftermath of the 1967 war, even the suspension of the flow of oil was not used as a political weapon for more than a few days.

Social justice was admittedly wanting all over the Arab world, but no one would have expected it to arouse such a militant crusade as could be aroused by the threat of a foreign intervention. Moreover, fighting for social justice, in contrast to fighting a foreign enemy, is essentially a local problem for which every country had to find its own particular solution and its own source of inspiration.

The ideal of Arab unity was also insufficient. Economists may go on for ever pointing out the advantages of a wider market and the greater bargaining power of a unified state. But these economic advantages may apply as much to Iraq's joining Kuwait as to her joining Iran or Turkey. Similarly, no amount of literature or speeches on the political advantages of a unified state can by themselves, generate a strong nationalist movement in the absence of an obvious foreign threat. A strong nationalist movement generated by such a threat may, however, be a powerful instrument in bringing about an economic as well as a political union.

But what probably proved to be the biggest blow to the Arab nationalist movement was the erosion of the ground on which the policy of "positive neutrality" had been built. By the early 1960's it had become clear that the game in which Nasser had been engaged since 1955 of playing off one foreign power against another, could no longer continue and Arab governments were forced to rely exclusively on one of the two super-powers. There is some evidence that Nasser did for some time try to resist it and to rely on his country's own material and human resources, but for both external and internal reasons this course seems to have been closed to him. Even if the political and economic interests of the super-powers could have been assumed to allow it, such a course would have required the loosening of political control and the elimination of the economic privileges of the governing élites to a degree which neither Nasser nor any other Arab ruler, was prepared to grant.

Ironically, but significantly, as Nasser grew increasingly dependent on the Soviet Union, he also became increasingly willing to effect a rapprochement with Arab monarchs whom, in his few years of independence, he had called reactionary. National dignity seemed to be divisible so that while the Arabs came to be repeatedly told that they were indeed "liberated" from the domination of one power, they were at the same time continuously urged to be grateful to the other. If their countries were defeated at war it was to be generously admitted by Arab governments that the fault was not that of any one but their own people. And the people believed it.

CHAPTER THREE

NEW INEQUALITIES FOR OLD

Underdeveloped countries have shown no less inclination to import academic fashions from the West than to import its goods. Just as the subject of income distribution went out of fashion in Western academic circles some twenty years ago, so it also lost its attraction to Arab economists. Concentration came instead to be on the problems of raising per capita income of the country as a whole.

This is indeed regrettable, for if the advanced countries have on the whole succeeded in eliminating, or at least in greatly reducing, the worst forms of personal and regional inequality this has by no means been achieved by any Arab country.

Arab statistics on income distribution are, significantly, among the most deficient, and when they do exist are among the most difficult to obtain. Available estimates, however rough, indicate a degree of inequality of personal distribution of income comparable to that prevailing in other underdeveloped countries such as India, Ceylon or Mexico, but considerably higher than those prevailing in Western Europe and the U.S.A.[1]

Some Western economists have expressed their dissatisfaction with a criterion of social welfare from which income distribution is excluded, and which regards any increase in aggregate output as desirable so long as the gainers could, but not necessarily would, compensate the losers.[2]

---

[1] See Table 29. Other available estimates for the late 1950's indicate that the poorest 20% of the population receive less than 6% of total national income in the *Sudan*, 2% in *Iraq*, 3% in *Lebanon* and only about one tenth of one percent in *Libya*. For *Lebanon* the IFRED mission estimated that the poorer half of the population received, in 1960, less than one fifth of national income, while the richest fifth received more than 60%. Again for *Libya* a recent estimate (1968) gives the figure of 50% of total disposable income as accruing to the top 10% of total population. For *Syria* in 1956-69, 75% of total population was estimated to receive 25% of national income and to have a per capita income of about £S. 170 per annum (about $ 45). For *Egypt* 52% of national income was estimated to accrue to under 10% of the population in 1958. (See: Adelman, I. and Morris, C.: An Anatomy of Income Distribution in Developing Countries, excerpt published in *Development Digest*, Oct. 1971, p. 27; Hilan, R.: *Culture et Développement en Syrie et dans les Pays Retardés*, Editions Anthropos, Paris, 1969, p. 228; Farley, *op. cit.*, p. 64 & 227; Beydoun, *op. cit.*, p. 180; and U.N.: *Report on the World Social Situation*, 1963.)

[2] See for example, Little, I.: *A Critique of Welfare Economics*, Oxford, 1950, pp. 92-8.

Table 29

Percentages of National Income received by the 5% of Total Population with Highest Income, in the Late 1950's

Country	%	*Country*	%
Lebanon	34	Syria	more than 33 [b]
Iraq	34	Libya	46
Egypt	more than 34 [a]	Sudan	17
U.S.A. (1950)	20.4	India (1950)	33
Britain (1951-2)	20.9	Ceylon (1952-3)	31
W. Germany (1950)	23.6	Mexico (1957)	37
Denmark (1957)	20.1		
Netherlands (1950)	24.6		

[a] Percentage of the total income of urban population only accruing to the top 5% of urban population.

[b] Percentage of total national income accruing to the top 5% of urban population only.

Sources: Lebanon, Iraq, Libya and Sudan: Adelman & Morris, *op. cit.*, p. 27; *Egypt:* Riad, H.: *L'Égypte Nasserienne*, Les Éditions de Minuit, Paris, 1964, p. 41; *Syria:* Hilan, *op. cit.*, p. 228. *Other countries:* Gannage, G.: The Distribution of Income in Underdeveloped Countries, in Marchal, J. & Ducros, B. (eds.): *The Distribution of National Income*, Macmillan, N.Y., 1968, p. 346.

But if it is fanciful to suppose that some redistributive mechanism operates in a developed country by means of which the poor is compensated for being made poorer during the process of growth, it is much more fanciful to make such an assumption in poor countries where the "spread effects" of growth are much more limited, where income taxes are much less effective, and where social benefits are heavily concentrated in a few cities.[3] In fact there are strong reasons to believe that, at least in some of the nine Arab countries, personal as well as regional income inequalities have increased with the rise in per capita income over the last two decades.

Twenty years ago the two main sources of income inequality in the Arab world were the domination of foreign economic interests and

[3] Apart from the income tax levied on the oil companies, the main source of revenue for Arab governments are indirect taxes. In many Arab countries no general income tax exists and where it does, its rates are less steep than those of the United States. This last statement is true even of Egypt, where income-tax rates are much steeper than in any other Arab country. The evasion of taxes levied on commercial and industrial profits as well as on incomes from the professions is generally high especially in Lebanon where, according to informed estimates, the rate of tax evasion runs in the neighbourhood of 66%. Taxes on wages and salaries are however easily ascertained and deducted at source.

inequality of land ownership. A third source of inequality may be added for Lebanon but had no comparable counterpart in other Arab countries, namely the confessional dichotomy of Lebanese society whereby most businessmen, and hence most of Lebanon's rich, were, as they still are, Christians.[4] Since then Arab countries have succeeded in reducing the strength of these factors, but new ones have been working with increasing force towards greater inequality. Of these new factors the most important seem to be the increase in oil revenue, the growth of government bureaucracy and a government bias against agriculture.

1. *Land Tenure and Foreign Economic Interests*

Outside agriculture and petty trade the Arab economy of 1950 was largely controlled by foreigners. Together with minority groups they controlled finance, manufacturing, foreign trade, a large part of internal trade ande often even the public utilities and the professions. In some cases, as that of Libya, foreigners even provided most of the skilled labour and monopolized the modern section of agriculture.[5]

On the other hand, in all except Saudi Arabia, Kuwait and the Sudan, the biggest 2% of all landowners owned or held a proportion of total cultivated land ranging from about one seventh in Egypt to about two thirds in Lebanon.[6] In the other three countries, inequality in the owner-

[4] In a study of entrepreneurs in Lebanon conducted in 1958, out of 207 entrepreneurs chosen mainly on the basis of their "innovating quality in their field" 166 were found to be Christians compared with only 34 moslems, 4 Jews and 3 druzes. In industry alone the number of Christians and moslems were 105 and 21 respectively, in finance 11 and 2, and in services 40 and 7. (See Y. Sayigh: *Entrepreneurs of Lebanon*, Harvard University Press, Cambridge, Massachusetts, 1962, p. 70. See also Issawi, Charles: Economic Development and Liberalism in Lebanon, *Middle East Journal*, Summer 1964, p. 289).

[5] See Issawi, Charles: The Arab World's Heavy Legacy, in Thompson & Reischauer (eds.), *op. cit.*, pp. 20-21.

[6] In Syria $2\frac{1}{2}$% of the total number of landowners held about 45% of irrigated and 30% of rainfed land while about 70% of the rural population did not own any land at all. About two thirds of Syria's big landowners were absentee landlords most of whom were not themselves farmers but merchants who invested their profits in agricultural land. However, the appropriator of the lion's share of agricultural income in Syria was not always the landowner, but varied from one agricultural region to another with variations in the relative scarcity of factors of production. In areas where rain is scarce the owner of a pump could get between 45 and 60% of the crop simply in return for the water he provided. Where rain and labour were abundant the landowner could get half the crop for providing the land, while in the Gezira, where land was abundant compared with labour, the lion's share went to the owners of tractors. (See Garzouzi, G.: Land Reform in Syria, *Middle East Journal*, Winter-Spring, 1963, p. 83; Warriner, D.: *Land Reform and Economic Development in the Middle East*, Oxford, 1962, Ch. 3; Berger, M.: *The Arab World Today*, Anchor Books, 1964, p. 197; Farley, *op. cit.*, pp. 137-8 and IBRD: *Economic Development of Syria*, *op. cit.*, p. 37).

ship of agricultural land constituted a much less serious problem either because the country had virtually no agriculture (Kuwait) or because land was under the collective control of the whole tribe, village or state, or was held by a broad class of small landholders, as in the Sudan and Saudi Arabia.[7]

Foreign economic predominance has since greatly declined in importance, so that outside the oil sector it is now important only in Lebanon.

The success of Arab countries in dealing with the other main source of inequality is much less obvious. For while no land reform on a national scale was introduced in Jordan or Lebanon,[8] the land reform laws of Egypt, Syria and Iraq were more effective in achieving their political aims than in reducing income inequality in the countryside. This is particularly true of Iraq and Syria. In the two countries both the expropriation of land and its redistribution have been far too slow. The whole 1958 land reform program of Iraq was supposed to be completed in five years. By 1963 only 12% of the land subject to distribution had actually been distributed. By mid-1969 out of 3.7 million hectares that had officially been estimated to fall under the terms of the law only 815,000 hectares (or 21.6%) had been actually requisitioned and distributed while more than 1.3 million hectares were being held by the land reform authorities. Much of the latter area has been temporarily rented to peasants, often by

---

[7] In the Sudan individual landownership is concentrated mainly in the riverain areas and covers about 6 million feddans, i.e., no more than 1% of the total area of the Sudan. The rest is owned by the state, about 40% of which is communally held by a tribe or a village community. Even in privately owned land the tenant has a status which is nearly equal to that of the proprietor-cultivator. As a result, and in contrast to Egypt, Syria and Iraq, neither the military nor the democratic governments of the Sudan were pressed to introduce land reform. Similarly, in Saudi Arabia the more widespread form of landholding is that of communal land tenure whereby the land is considered the property of the whole tribe or of an extended family whose members share the produce together. For the land which is individually owned large ownership is not common and rarely exceeds 40 acres. (See Awad, M. H.: The Evolution of Landownership in the Sudan, *Middle East Journal*, Spring, 1971, pp. 212-28; Raoof, A. H.: The Kingdom of Saudi Arabia, in Ismael, T.: *Governments and Politics of the Contemporary Middle East*, The Dorsey Press, Illinois, 1970, p. 358).

[8] Lebanon has not yet known a land reform and in the early 1960's more than half the cultivated land was still owned by 5% of all landowners. Jordan's land reform was undertaken mainly in the case of the East Ghor Canal development projects and did not cover the whole country. The influx of Palestinian refugees resulted in an increase in the share of rent in farm income by about 150% between 1948 and the early 1960's. (Lebanon's Ministry of Agriculture: *Agriculture in the Lebanese Economy* (mimeo.), 1968, p. 19; Clawson, M., Landsberg, H. & Alexander, L.: *The Agricultural Potential of the Middle East*, American Elsevier Publishing Company, N.Y., 1971, p. 225 and U.N.: *Report on the World Social Situation*, 1963).

one-year permits, until distribution is effected. The lack of security given to the peasants as well as the inadequacy of credit, tractors and irrigation facilities provided to them often led to cultivators abandoning the land.[9]

In Syria expropriation and redistribution have been obstructed by the continuous change of governments. The original land reform law of September 1958 was repealed and replaced by another in February 1962. In May of the same year it was again repealed and replaced by a legislative decree which reinstituted the 1958 law with minor modifications. In June 1963 a new decree abolished the 1962 modifications of the 1958 law, and introduced new ones. Syria's land reform, in contrast to that of Egypt's, also suffered from the lack of a sufficient number of trained officials who could carry out the necessary surveys and distribution, from the difficulty of applying the distinction made in the law between irrigated and rainfed land and from the inadequacy of cadastral surveys which often made it difficult to be certain about how much land one owned. Estimates of the area subject to expropriation in Syria could therefore vary from one to two and a half million hectares or from 20% to nearly 50% of cultivated area.[10] At the end of 1965, the area of land which had actually been expropriated was 1.2 million hectares of which only 708,000 were announced by the government to have been distributed by 1969.[11] In both Syria and Iraq the establishment of agricultural cooperatives has been equally slow.[12]

Thus, although the Egyptian land reform of 1952 was less radical on paper than those of Syria and Iraq in terms of the proportion of cultivated area subject to expropriation, it had a greater effect on peasants' income just as it was less damaging to productivity. But even for Egypt, the redistributive effects of land reform could be exaggerated. Writing in 1970, Doreen Warriner summarized these effects as follows:

> "although the law of 1952 brought a revolutionary change, the scope of redistribution under it was quite small. Its immediate effect was to raise

---

[9] Economist Intelligence Unit: *Iraq*, Annual Supplement, 1971, p. 10; Hamadi, S.: *Towards a Socialist Land Reform* (Arabic), Beirut, 1964, p. 11 and Clawson & others, *op. cit.*, p. 61.

[10] Wickmar, W.: *Modernization of Administration in the Near East*, Beirut, Khayat, 1963, p. 71.

[11] Wazzan, S.: *From Backwardness to Socialist Development in the Agricultural Sector* (Arabic), Damascus, 1967, pp. 224-36 and Economist Intelligence Unit: *Syria, Lebanon & Cyprus*, Annual Supplement, 1971, pp. 7-8.

[12] Less than 10% of all Syrian farmers belonged to cooperatives by the end of 1965 and about a fifth in Iraq in 1968.

> the incomes of a small proportion of the farm population on a small proportion of the cultivated area. Six other laws were later passed, one in 1961 reducing the original maximum holding of 200 acres to 100, others expropriating foreign-owned and other categories of land. Under these seven laws ... the area distributed amounted to about 12% of the total area in cultivation while the number of recipients represented about 10% of total farm population ... Apart from the larger holdings, where some control is exercised, the number and nature of leasing arrangements render (the) enforcement (of the legislation controlling rents and conditions of tenancy) impossible, as is always the case where the supply of labour greatly exceeds labour requirements. Minimum wage enforcement proved impossible for the same reason." [13]

If the Egyptian bureaucracy has proved more effective than that of Iraq or Syria in implementing the expropriation and redistribution of land, as well as in performing the functions previously performed by the landlords it has also shown a greater tendency to inherit their power. It took only four years for the High Committee for Land Reform to which the implementation of the 1952 law was first entrusted, to grow into the General Organization of Land Reform, thought at the time to dissolve once redistribution was completed, and finally into the Ministry of Land Reform, permanently established for a growing absentee bureaucracy in Cairo. A few of them occupied the mansions of the expropriated landlords while the *mushrifs* (the cooperative supervisors) replaced the ex-landlords' bailiffs and are often referred to by the peasants with the same term: *nazir al-ziraat*. These mushrifs, according to G. Saab, are most of the time "only concerned with the problem of obtaining as promptly as possible the settlement of the land taxes, annual instalments, and loans in kind or cash due by the members (of the cooperatives). Permanently on the alert to detect some new means of mopping up outstanding debts (often the result of the high level of instalments and rents), the efforts of the *mushrifs* therefore concentrated more on short-term objectives directly related to this rather than on the introduction of thorough and radical changes in the techniques and ways of life of the peasantry in their care. Active supervision of agricultural operations was confined principally to the crops disposed of through cooperative channels since this provided an easy way of collecting debts..." [14]

[13] Warriner, D.: *Land Reform, Income and Employment in the Middle East, International Labour Review*, June 1970, p. 615. Dr. Warriner does not refer to the 1969 landreform law which further reduced the maximum holding per family to 100 feddans and individual ownership to 50 feddans. By 1971, however, only 850,000 feddans had been redistributed out of a total cultivated area of about 5.9 million feddans or 14.4%.

[14] Saab, G.: *The Egyptian Agrarian Reform (1952-62)*, Oxford University Press, 1967, pp. 54-5 and 70.

According to a study conducted six years after the first land reform law, an Egyptian peasant who received land according to this law could be paying almost £E 50 per year for each feddan: 14.45 as an annual instalment, 12.06 for irrigation facilities . . . etc., 10 for farm supplies and 10 to pay off earlier loans and other minor charges. Another estimate made in the same year showed that the various disbursements incurred by a peasant to the land-reform authorities could exceed his income.[15]

Another field study of two sample land-reform estates, Demira and Nabaroh in the Dakahliya province, has recently concluded that "the net income per recipient in the two sample estates was not only below that of a tenant farmer in the same estates during 1950-2 but also below the national average income per tenant in 1956-63." [16]

Early in 1953 the new Egyptian regime announced its commitment to a general program of rural reform and development which came to be known as the "Combined Units' Project". In each of some 868 areas inhabited by the rural population of about 13 million a "combined unit" was to be created including a complete health centre, child-welfare centre, centre for expectant mothers, an assembly hall, a museum, a school, a nursery, five villas for married officials as well as dwellings for 24 bachelor officials. According to the optimistic estimates of the Permanent Council for Public Welfare Services, the 868 combined units were to be completed by 1960. In 1955 President Nasser inaugurated the first combined unit in a village in the Giza Province. By 1960, however, only 250 units had been built. The first five-year plan indicated that by 1970 over 500 combined units would be functioning but by the spring of 1967 a total of only 301 combined units could be verified.

The government blamed this on "the lack of funds and of qualified personnel". But more important than the sheer number of buildings is the fact that other than those combined units located in the governorates just outside of Cairo, which appear to operate mainly as a model for foreign visitors, the buildings of the combined units are very poorly equipped, while many are largely deserted. A study published in 1965 and conducted by the Egyptian Institute of National Planning in cooperation with the I.L.O. was based on interviews from a random sample of 994

---

[15] See Abdel-Malek, A.: *Egypt: Military Society*, Vintage Books, N.Y., 1968, p. 73.

[16] Abdel-Khalek, M.: *Agrarian Reform in Egypt, A Field Study of the Agrarian Reform in Two Typical Areas During the Period 1953-63*, Unpublished Ph.D. thesis, London University, 1971, p. III. The same writer goes on to say that "the Agrarian Reform Authority either distorted the statistics or deliberately published some statistics relating only to a number of fields in selected areas or did not publish any statistics at all, as in the case of Nabaroh," p. 268.

rural households chosen from 48 "typical villages" in six different governorates. In these interviews the head of each household was asked whether "he or his family had received any benefits from administrative services available in their village." The percentages of negative responses were 26% for health, 73% for education, 76% for agricultural services, 82% for veterinary and agricultural extension services and 98% for vocational training.[17]

2. *Oil Revenue and Income Distribution*

Before the arrival of the oil companies the virtual absence of industry in Kuwait and Saudi Arabia, combined with the tradition of collective land ownership and the strong influence of Wahabism in the latter, have ensured a degree of income and social equality rarely known in the under-developed world. Even the slaves in Arabia could hardly have been distinguished from free men performing the same tasks. The flow of oil revenue has since then contributed to the liberation of slaves by bringing enough income to their masters to pay for other forms of service and to the government to pay for their release.[18] But the flow of oil has also made possible the importation of luxury goods as well as guns.

Feeling their new superiority the rulers no longer accepted to be called by their first names, as was the custom in Arabia, nor to live in the same sun-dried brick huts as their subjects. Before Saudi Arabia's doors were opened to Western influence, Quranic jurisdiction was applied to all, and however severe the punishment of chopping off the thief's hand may seem to Western eyes it may not have appeared so severe to the people of Arabia where such a high degree of equality as well as poverty prevailed. Such punishment could not obviously have been applied to the foreigners who were coming to Saudi Arabia in increasing numbers, nor could it easily be defended in the new society where income inequalities were growing and attractive Western goods were being consumed and envied. The inevitable outcome was the rise of class justice, where the poor Saudis remained subject to Quranic jurisdiction while foreigners as well as the more westernized Saudis received much milder punishment.[19]

---

[17] See Mayfield, J.: *Rural Politics in Nasser's Egypt*, University of Texas Press, Austin, 1971, pp. 177-185.

[18] Holden, *op. cit.*, p. 136.

[19] Van Der Meulen reported that the Americans in Saudi Arabia, horrified by the severity of some punishments tended to avoid reporting Saudi subjects to their police with the result of a marked deterioration in their conduct. (*The Wells of Ibn Saud*, *op. cit.*, pp. 253-4).

Until the mid-1960's the main instrument used by the Kuwaiti government to disburse its revenue from oil to the private sector was the land-purchase program according to which the government bought, at highly inflated prices, privately owned land which was then either used for development projects or resold to private buyers. About $ 1.7 billion was estimated to have been transferred in this manner up to 1969. Apart from the fact that the greatest part of the sum received in this way by the private sector was invested abroad, so that its effect on economic activity at home was insignificant, the program tended to increase income inequality since those who benefitted from it were relatively few in number and they subsequently realized big capital gains from the increase in land value. Urban land that was worthless twenty years ago is now among the most high-priced in the world; yet no capital gains tax was introduced.[20]

Nomads and semi-nomads, who still constitute between a fifth to a fourth of total population in Libya and Saudi Arabia, have been almost completely isolated from any educational or medical services and are hardly aware of their belonging to a nation-state. Their main gain from oil was perhaps that sometimes during the search for oil, water was found instead.

Lower-income groups have particularly suffered in Libya from an excessive rise in prices. The strong inflationary pressure of the late 1950's continued after the discovery of oil as a result of the heavy government expenditure on infrastructure, that of oil companies on pipelines, terminals and other forms of construction as well as the weak response of agriculture. Retail food prices doubled between 1955 and 1967 and in one year 1966-67 the cost of living rose by about 17%. In the face of such a high rate of inflation the Lybian government has been highly inactive. It refrained from taking measures towards reforming the fiscal system by taxing the easily reaped profits, it failed to encourage investment in the more productive sectors, nor did it make use of government borrowing. The only direct taxes continued to be the annual 10% flat-rate income tax on commercial profits and the 8% tax levied on wage-earners. In its report on the first five-year plan (1963-68), the Development Council advised the government to set up a high-powered committee to investigate the necessary measures for combating inflation. This committee, how-

[20] El-Mallakh, R.: *Economic Development and Regional Cooperation: Kuwait*, *op. cit.*, pp. 75-6; Asfour, E.: *op. cit.*, p. 389 and IBRD: *The Economic Development of Kuwait*, *op. cit.*, p. 4 & 28.

ever, never met, nor was a comprehensive anti-inflationary policy ever drawn up.[21]

3. *Government Bureaucracy*

One further result of the flow of oil revenue as well as of foreign aid directly into the hands of Arab governments was the rapid growth of the public sector and of government administration. Additional factors in countries governed by the military were the advocation of "Arab Socialism", the insatiable desire to sell the revolution to the masses, as well as the new governments' fear of the political consequences of unemployment among the educated.

Thus the rate of growth of the civil service was no less than 15% per annum in Syria (1964-66) and Egypt (1962/3-66/7).[22] At the same time that the Egyptian government was declaring its aim to make administration more efficient it was announcing its intention of finding jobs for most of the 26000 new university graduates looking for work in 1965, a 'revolutionary' version of an ethic of a poor society. In the Sudan, the main public corporation beside the Gezira scheme, namely the Sudan Railways, which monopolises railroads and steamers and operates hotel and catering services, is the largest employer of labour in the country. But the rapid growth of the civil service is not confined to countries with military governments. In Saudi Arabia the number of civilian employees increased by 120% in six years (1959-65) and by 1967, about 30% of the total employed (excluding the armed forces) were government employees. The corresponding percentage for Kuwait was 40% in 1965, and now almost one of every six persons living in Kuwait is on the government payroll.[23]

Twenty years ago public ownership rarely extended beyond irrigation works and public utilities and the government's share in total expenditure did not exceed one fifth of GNP except in some of the oil countries. By the mid-1960's this ratio had increased by 50% in Jordan, 80% in Iraq and more than doubled in Egypt, Syria and Kuwait.[24] Outside agriculture,[25] oil, retail trade, housing and small-scale industry the public sector

[21] See El-Mallakh, R.: The Economics of Rapid Growth: Libya, *Middle East Journal*, Summer, 1969, p. 315; Farley, *op. cit.*, p. 230 and Abu-Saud, *op. cit.*, pp. 88-9.

[22] Hansen, B.: *Economic Development in Syria*, *op. cit.*, p. VI, and Ghoneim, A.: The New Class in Egypt, in *Al-Taliaa*, February, 1968.

[23] Ismael, *op. cit.*, p. 370; Asfour, *op. cit.*, p. 374 & 384 and El-Mallakh, *op. cit.*, p. 78.

[24] See Table 30.

[25] In the Sudan, however, the Gezira scheme, which occupies a little less than one fourth of all of Sudan's land under crop production (both irrigated and rainfed) is run as a public corporation.

is now predominant in Egypt, Iraq and Syria and is fast growing in all except Lebanon. Outside Lebanon and Jordan [26] the share of public investment is nowhere less than 50% and it is more than 75% in Iraq and Egypt. Even "traditional" Saudi Arabia has gone a long way since the state itself was a private enterprise. Public investment has been rising in Saudi Arabia in recent years twice as fast as private investment (20% and 9% a year respectively) so that the two are now roughly equal.[27] The General Petroleum and Mineral Organization (PETROMIN) established in Saudi Arabia in 1962 and charged with the task of diversifying the economy, is a state-owned corporation. Only in Lebanon is the role of the state still confined to public utilities [28] and, ideological slogans apart, Lebanon is the only true citadel of private enterprise which remains in the Arab world.

Table 30

Government Expenditures as % of GNP

Country	*Year*	%	*Country*	*Year*	%
Lebanon	1965	21	S. Arabia	1966	40
Sudan	1965	23	Syria	1966	41
Iraq	1965	29	Kuwait	1966	47
Jordan	1967	36	Egypt	1966	55

Source: Issawi, Charles: Growth and Structural Change in Middle East, *Middle East Journal*, Summer, 1971, pp. 320-1.

In all the nine countries the higher ranks of government officials constitute a privileged group whose rewards, especially if the non-monetary ones are included, are more often than not, out of proportion with their services. Their offices and houses tend to be lavishly furnished, they are generously provided with free trips abroad and both they and their families have easy access to the country's foreign exchange. While their high level of consumption is taken for granted in the oil countries, Jordan and Lebanon it seems to be positively encouraged by military governments. Lacking the support of a land-owning or capitalist class

[26] In the mid-1960's the share of public investment in total gross investment was 43% in Jordan and less than one fifth in Lebanon.

[27] Issawi, *Growth and Structural Change in the Middle East*, *op. cit.*, p. 313.

[28] Even this exaggerates the role of the Lebanese government, considering that many public utilities are still privately owned and run, such as a good part of the means of transport and the only two television stations. Even money issue and control was run until 1964 as a concession by a private bank which assumed the role of Lebanon's central bank.

the new governments tend to favour the rise of a new class which, never before having such a taste of power and luxury, find its personal interest at one with that of the new regime. Even in Egypt, where redistribution of income in favour of the lower classes has gone further than in any other Arab country, it has been amply shown [29] that those who benefitted most from "Arab Socialism" were the higher ranks of government officials, the managers and the army officers as well as the small fraction of labour force employed in corporate enterprises. The total pay of Egyptian top government officials has been increasing much more rapidly than the total salaries and wages of the lower ranks. According to state budgets, between 1962/3 and 1966/7 total salaries in government administration as well as public companies and organizations increased by 77% while the salaries and "representation allowances" paid to the higher ranks in central government administration [30] increased by as much as 146% during the same period. In 1966/7 the total annual salaries as well as representation allowances paid to the top 1085 jobs in central government administration amounted to £E. 2.578 million, the average annual income being £E. 2376 or about 40 times the per capita income of the whole population.[31] A not untypical chairman of the board of directors in a public company gets about £E. 2000 as a basic salary, 1500 as representation allowances, 125 as travel allowances plus 600 as his annual share in bonuses and profits, the total being £E. 4225 per annum.[32] According to the scale of salaries included in the Presidential Decree No. 3309/1966 the ratio between the highest salary, excluding representation allowances (£E. 1900-2000) and the lowest (£E. 60-84) in government administration and the public sector is 27 : 1. If representation allowances for the highest grade is included the ratio may exceed 40 : 1.[33] This is to be compared with a ratio between the salaries of top grades of the civil service and the wage of an average unskilled labourer in Britain of about 5 : 1 before and 4 : 1 after tax.

4. *The Bias Against Agriculture*

Development economists are now agreed that in order for industrializa-

[29] See O'Brien, P.: *The Revolution in Egypt's Economic System*, Oxford University Press, 1966; Riad, H.: *L'Égypte Nasserienne*, Les Éditions de Minuit, Paris, 1964 and Abdel-Malek, A.: *Egypt: Military Society*, Vintage Books, N.Y., 1968.

[30] Numbering 733 jobs in 1962/3 and 1085 in 1966/7 (see Ghoneim, A., *op. cit.*, p. 91).

[31] Calculated from *ibid.*, p. 89.

[32] El-Said, R.: The Role of the Middle Class in the Egyptian Society, *Al-Taliaa*, March 1972, p. 69.

[33] Ghoneim, *op. cit.*, p. 90.

tion to succeed, agricultural output has to grow at a comparable rate, and that failure to achieve this may constitute the most important obstacle to industrial growth. A more obvious, but no less important, justification for aiming at a high rate of growth in Arab agriculture is that more than half the Arab population relies directly on it for its livelihood. In most Arab countries the average rate of growth of agricultural output over the last two decades has been less than half that of manufacturing.[34]

In Saudi Arabia and Libya, oil has not only failed to pull forward the production of agriculture and animal husbandry but has actually contributed to their decline.[35] This has been partly due to the increasing sedentarization of nomads and to the increasing competition of well-paid and more stable employment with the oil companies or the government. Yet many more labourers have emigrated to the towns than could be absorbed by either, and had more attention been given to agriculture many of these might have remained on the land without a labour shortage being felt in the towns. Water seems to be available[36] but it is misused

---

[34] Available agricultural data indicate an annual rate of growth of agricultural output in *Saudi Arabia* (1963-69) of 1.7% compared with 12.1% for manufacturing and 7.9% for GDP. In *Libya* (1962-67) the annual rate of growth of agriculture was 4.5% compared with 28% for GDP, 30% for construction and over 20% for services. After achieving remarkable progress in the early post-war years, *Syria's* agricultural output grew at an average annual rate of only 1.3% between 1956 and 1968, to which Hansen attributes the decline in Syria's over-all rate of growth after 1956. The performance of *Egyptian* agriculture also tended to deteriorate, so that, compared with about 10% increase in per capita agricultural output over the 1950's, it remained more or less constant between 1960 and 1965 and subsequently declined. No data is available for *Kuwait* except for 1966-68 during which an annual rate of decline of 15% was reported (including fishing and pearling). Iraq, Lebanon and the Sudan show different performances in different periods, from an annual rate of growth of 2.7% (1955-60) to 7.8% (1960-68) in *Iraq*; and from 2.0% (1950-57) to 6.9% (1957-64) and 3.3% (1964-68) in *Lebanon*, and from 2.7% (1955-60) to 10.3% (1960-64) in the *Sudan*. The highest rate was that of *Jordan* (12.5% at current prices between 1959 and 1968). (Sources: U.N.: *Yearbook of National Accounts Statistics*, 1969; UNESOB: *La Croissance Économique*, *op. cit.*, p. 57 & 276-9; Hansen, B.: *Economic Development in Syria*, *op. cit.*, p. 11; Economist Intelligence Unit: *Saudi Arabia & Jordan*, No. 1, 1971, p. 7; Farley, *op. cit.*, p. 244 and FAO: *Production Yearbook*, 1969).

[35] Before the exploitation of oil both Saudi Arabia and Libya were net exporters of livestock. Since then the decline in animal husbandry has turned them into net importers. By the late 1960's the total value of exports of food and live animals of both countries constituted no more than 1% of their imports of the same items. Primary non-oil exports other than food, such as Libya's exports of esparto grass (used in the paper industry) and sponges, have also dwindled.

[36] Compared with the present area under cultivation in Saudi Arabia of less than one million acres (about 0.2% of the country's total area) an American estimate gives 15% of the total area of Saudi Arabia as potentially cultivable. The IBRD mission to Libya has also reported large possibilities for developing Libya's water resources. (See Economist Intelligence Unit: *Saudi Arabia and Jordan*, Annual Supplement, 1971,

or neglected, either because of the existing tribal rights or because little has been invested by the government in the digging of new wells or in the preservation of flood waters.[37] A similar neglect of pearling and fishing could be observed in Kuwait.[38]

Table 31

Saudi Arabia: Financial Allocations in the Five-Year Plan (1970-75) (Percentages)

Administration	18.6
Defence	23.1
Education	17.8
Health and Social Affairs	4.7
Public Utilities and Urban Development	11.1
Transport and Communications	18.1
Industry	2.7
Agriculture	3.6
Trade and Services	0.3
Total	100.0

Source: Economist Intelligence Unit: *Saudi Arabia and Jordan*, Annual Supplement, 1971, p. 14.

In Lebanon, the government has not shown particular zeal in making credit available to small farmers, while the banking system has provided much less credit to agriculture than to either industry, building or commerce (see Table 32).

In 1955 a new bank was established in Lebanon under the name of the Bank of Agricultural, Industrial and Financial Credit (B.C.A.I.F.) and was described by the IFRED mission in 1961 as "the only credit organiza-

p. 4; IBRD: *The Economic Development of Libya*, *op. cit.*, p. 26. See also Farley, *op. cit.*, pp. 242-3 & 133; Allan, J.: Some Recent Developments in Libyan Agriculture, *Middle East Economic Papers*, 1969 and UNESOB: *Studies on Selected Development Problems*, 1968, p. 33).

[37] See Table 31. In 1965 the Monetary Agency of Saudi Arabia established the Agricultural Bank to provide farmers with loans for the purchase of engines, pumps and livestock. During the following five years the total value of loans provided by this bank was 53.5 million S. Riyals, the annual average being less than 7% of the annual allocations to the Royal Treasury (173 million). (Saudi Arabian Monetary Agency: *Annual Report*, 1388-89 A.H., p. 22).

In the 1968/9 development budget of Libya, agriculture, animal resources and forests were allotted £L. 11 million in addition to 5.3 million in the general budget, compared with 31.2 million allotted to the ministry of interior and 14.3 million to defence. (Farley, *op. cit.*, pp. 304-5).

[38] In 1912 Kuwait had more than 800 ships employed in pearling, by 1956 the number had declined to five. (El-Mallakh, *op. cit.*, p. 12).

Table 32

Lebanon: Loans Provided by the Banking System to Various Economic Sectors (£L. 000)

	1964	1965	1966	Dec. 1967	Dec. 1968
Agriculture	124,216	128,094	132,052	131,266	132,564
Industry	235,987	303,730	341,498	381,800	401,904
Building	141,051	206,536	212,142	229,387	248,979
Commerce:					
Foreign Trade	196,350	236,230	349,208	379,955	367,552
Internal Trade	546,580	667,919	563,757	548,768	542,354
Services	122,038	141,144	172,345	171,300	170,379
Consumption	122,445	135,995	157,387	140,382	126,643
Total Commerce	987,413	1,181,288	1,242,697	1,240,405	1,206,928
Finance	100,911	115,770	143,058	134,668	121,448
Other	248,916	275,771	251,821	237,867	236,647
Grand Total	1,838,494	2,211,189	2,323,268	2,355,393	2,348,470

Source: Keyrouz, K.: *Reflections on the Most Important Socio-Economic Problems of Contemporary Lebanon*, (Arabic), Lebanese University, Beirut, 1970, p. 127.

tion aiming at the development of the whole country." [39] The Government was to own 40% of its shares, the rest being left for other banks or individuals. Out of the average annual loans provided by this bank between 1955 and 1959 (£L. 114,000) less than 5% went to agriculture, and this "unfortunately went particularly to urban capitalists who wanted to create orchards with the likely result of dispossessing poor peasants." [40] The IFRED report went on to say that

> "usury is very widespread in agriculture; one competent person has described the Bekaa' as 'the land of usury'. It is not surprising if the inhabitants of that region do not regard a bank in Baalbeck, which charges an interest of 18% per annum as a great benefactor. Usury often forces the poor peasant to cultivate 'hashish', which clearly indicates that attack against its cultivation cannot make any sense if not coupled with a policy for supplying middle and long-term agricultural credit at less heavy terms." [41]

A project for the development of the use of the Litani river, Lebanon's most important source of water, for both irrigation and hydro-electricity was entrusted to a special government department as long ago as 1954. The development of hydro-electricity was carried out quite rapidly but

[39] IFRED: *Le Liban Face À Son Développement*, Beirut, 1963, p. 258.
[40] *Ibid.*
[41] *Ibid.*, p. 259.

that of irrigation has been much slower. By 1968 three hydroelectric stations had been completed but only one "model" irrigation project covering 1500 hectares. One writer explained this by the fact that "hydro-electric projects show more rapid profits than do agricultural ones, the former can be self-liquidating while the latter require a long-term investment policy", as well as by disagreements between the representatives of the different regions on the allocation of the water saved.[42]

In countries with more "radical" governments, the bias against agriculture did not take the form of depriving it of investment funds. In fact, in many of their plans, agriculture was given a greater share of total investments than industry.[43] The problem was rather that too great a share of public investments directed to agriculture has been in large-scale, capital-intensive irrigation projects. This is not to deny either the importance of the High Dam for Egypt, considering her population pressure on the land, or of the Euphrates Dam for Syria with her urgent need to reduce dependence on rainfall. However, in all the four countries: Egypt, Syria, Iraq and the Sudan, the construction of big irrigation projects has been at the expense of improving yields, which could have brought substantial returns and greater employment at less cost and in a much shorter time.[44] Moreover, while the construction of the Euphrates Dam was being delayed by the continuous changes in the Syrian government, Egypt was wasting large amounts of capital on the Tahrir Province and the New Valley schemes which, having ended in failure, are now hardly ever mentioned. In contrast to Iraq and Syria, however, Egypt should at least be credited with avoiding a decline in crop yields.[45] In

[42] Hudson, J.: The Litani River of Lebanon: An Example of Middle Eastern Water Development, *Middle East Journal*, Winter, 1971, pp. 11-2 and UNESOB, *op. cit.*, 1969, pp. 163-4 of the Arabic edition.

[43] In Iraq's plans, priority was given to agriculture over industry up to 1958, thereafter first priority was given to industry. Again, while in the earlier period (1951-58) the percentage of actual to planned investment in agriculture was 51.1% it became 36.6% in 1959-65. In the following three years (1966/7-1968/9) actual development expenditure on agriculture ranged between 19% and 33% of allocations made to agriculture in annual budgets. (Jalal, F., *op. cit.*, p. 47 & 65 and Economist Intelligence Unit: *Iraq, Annual Supplement*, 1971, p. 8).

[44] For an elaboration of this point see, for *Egypt*, Mohie-El-Dine, A.: *Agricultural Investment and Employment in Egypt Since 1935*, Unpublished Ph.D. thesis, London University, 1966 and for *Iraq*, Badre, A.: *Economic Development in Iraq*, in Cooper & Alexander(eds.), *op. cit.*, p. 292 and for *Sudan*, Wynn, *op. cit.*, pp. 574-5 and Osman, A.: *Planning Agricultural Policies and Policy Implementation in the Republic of the Sudan*, Unpublished Ph.D. thesis, Michigan State University, 1968, pp. 69-70.

[45] In *Syria* the net value added per hectare of cultivated land in 1963 was almost half its level in 1950 (both relatively normal years). By 1967 it had partly recovered but had not regained its 1950 level. In *Iraq* the average annual production of grain in

Iraq, although the area under cultivation has doubled since the second world war, little was done to improve credit and marketing facilities, to extend the use of fertilizers beyond the small area under cotton [46] nor, above all, to save the already cultivated land from increasing salination, which is by far the most serious single problem facing Iraqi agriculture. According to Dr M. Diab of the American University of Beirut, an Iraqi consultant engineer reported to him that a minister, in reply to the latter's plea for an allocation of financial resources to the provision of more adequate drainage facilities and less to dams said, "Everybody sees a dam, but who sees a drainage canal?" Another minister told him: "A dam could be inaugurated, but who would wish to inaugurate a drainage network?" [47]

In the Sudan, agricultural progress has been heavily concentrated in the relatively small modern sector which lies almost exclusively in the area between the two Niles south of Khartoum, to the neglect of traditional agriculture which supports no less than two thirds of the population. Within the traditional sector the southern provinces, inhabited by about a third of total population, have been the most discriminated against both economically and socially. Upon Sudan's independence in 1956 the Gezira, together with the Gash-Tokar region, employed only 8% of Sudan's labour force but earned about a fifth of national income. Low as per capita income was for the Sudan as a whole, per capita income in the Three Towns, where most of the population of the modern sector is concentrated, was estimated to be about 12 times that of a typical animal owner in Southern Sudan.[48] Since independence these disparities have increased. In the six years following independence the rate of growth of GDP of the modern sector was more than three times that of the tradition-

---

1962-66 was about 10% below the 1954-58 average. No such decline in yields has occurred in *Egypt* where some crop yields have on the contrary shown considerable improvement. With a much less urgent drainage problem than Iraq, Egypt made greater progress in this field. Thus the yield per feddan in 1967-68 was 95% higher than the 1950-1 average for wheat, 67% for maize and 40% for rice. But no such big increase is recorded for cotton especially during the last decade. (Hansen: *Economic Development in Syria*, pp. 21-2; Warriner, D.: *Land Reform, Income and Employment in the Middle East, op. cit.*, pp. 618-9 and National Bank of Egypt: *Economic Bulletin*, 1970, No. I).

[46] See Stickley, S. and others (eds.): *Man, Food and Agriculture in the Middle East*, American University of Beirut, 1969, p. 181.

[47] Diab, M.: *Environmental Considerations in the Management of Natural Resources in the Middle East*, A paper presented to UNESOB Regional Seminar on Development and Environment, Beirut, 1971 (mimeo.) p. 15.

[48] Mcloughlin, P.: The Sudan's Three Towns, Part II, Output and Expenditure, *Economic Development and Cultural Change*, Jan., 1964, p. 159.

al sector. Again in the ten-year plan (1960-70) a growth rate of 6.9% was projected for the modern sector while the traditional sector was scheduled to grow at the same pre-plan rate of 3.3%.[49] National policy continued, as was the case before independence, to concentrate on the improvement of the marketing of the cotton crop, which is predominantly produced in the modern sector. Fertilizers and insecticides are easily and cheaply accessible to the Gezira area where they are obtained in bulk at cost price, while the traditional cultivators obtain them, if at all, through intermediaries at much higher prices. Thus, the average yield per feddan of three main crops of traditional agriculture, sorghum, sesame and groundnuts were in 1964-66 between 15 and 20% lower than the 1960/1 level.[50] Discrimination against the Southerners also continued after independence. While the British service for the South was almost confined to abolishing the slave trade, educating a few in English and converting them to Christianity, national governments concentrated on replacing Christian by Islamic teaching rather than on providing the South with more schools.[51]

It may be argued that such a policy of concentrating investment in the modern sector is economically sound considering the extremely underdeveloped infrastructure in the rest of the economy. This view is not only difficult to defend on social grounds but may prove to have been shortsighted even from the economic point of view. In the first place, whatever gain may be reaped from higher returns on investments made in the modern sector may be lost by the demoralizing effect which such a policy of discrimination must have on the inhabitants of the traditional sector. Secondly, if such discrimination results, as it has in fact done, in the aggravation of tension between the two regions one must count among the losses the increase in military expenditure as well as the costs of political instability.[52] Thirdly, despite the more developed infrastructure of the northern region, it is by no means obvious that higher returns

[49] Osman, *op. cit.*, p. 69. Of total planned investment in agriculture, the share of traditional agriculture was 7.7%.

[50] *Ibid.*, pp. 164-6.

[51] Two projects for the exploitation of the agricultural resources of the South were abandoned by the government, one for building a sugar factory and another for the production of paper from the papyrus of the southern swamps. The two firms which were entrusted with the projects, one British and one German, had asked to establish the factories near the source of raw materials but the government insisted on establishing them in the North. (See Albino, O.: *The Sudan: A Southern Point of View*, Oxford, 1970, p. 90).

[52] According to Albino, (*op. cit.*, p. 93) the cost to the government of the "security operations" against rebellion in the South was £S. 2 million per month.

should in all cases have been reaped from building new factories there rather than in areas of traditional agriculture where factories may be nearer to the sources of raw materials. Nor is this necessarily more remunerative than developing the cultivation of cash crops in the south such as sugar-cane or coffee, or than increasing the production of livestock which is almost completely produced in traditional agriculture and has better export prospects than cotton.

A rough indicator of the differences between the level of living of the agricultural population and the rest is provided by Table 33. The disparity is particularly wide in the oil countries, other than Kuwait, and in Lebanon, where the service sector is exceptionally profitable. Thus, for example, while more than half the economically active population in Saudi Arabia are engaged in agricultural activities they contribute no more than one tenth of GDP. Similarly, Lebanon's service sector contributes as much as 70% of GDP but employs less than half the economically active population, whereas the agricultural sector contributes only 10% of GDP and supports about a third of the population.[53]

Table 33

The Share of Agriculture in Total Economically Active Population and in GDP in 1965

Country	*% of Economically Active Population*	*% of GDP*
Sudan	78	54
Saudi Arabia [a]	58	10
Syria [b]	58	28
Egypt	52	28
Iraq	42	19
Libya	35	5
Lebanon [c]	34	10
Jordan	33	16
Kuwait	1	.5

[a] 1963. [b] 1967. [c] 1968.

Sources: FAO: *Production Yearbook*, 1968; U.N.: *Yearbooks of National Accounts Statistics*; UNESOB: *La Croissance Économique, op. cit.*, pp. 84-5 & 229.

[53] According to another source, the ratio between per capita income of farm population and national average income was 48% in Egypt (1965), 41% in Lebanon (1958) and 57% in Iraq (1965) while in Jordan the ratio between value added per worker in agriculture and that in the whole economy was 56% in 1961 (Clawson, M., Landsberg, H. and Alexander, L.: *The Agricultural Potential of the Middle East*, p. 100). According to the Egyptian Family Budget survey of 1963/4 the percentage of the rural population whose total annual expenditure per family was £E. 100 or less was 48.8% compared

There is also some statistical evidence for the tendency of the gap between rural and urban average incomes to increase. Thus, an index of differential industrial and agricultural real wages in Egypt shows an increase of 54% between 1950 and 1961 compared with a decline of 15% during the period 1938-50.[54] For Iraq, an FAO report estimated the 1956 per capita income in the "non-oil" sector (which is likely to be higher than that of the agricultural population alone) at $ 105 compared with $ 135 as a national average. For 1965, an unpublished report of Iraq's Bureau of Statistics estimated the per capita income of the agricultural population as $ 123 [55] compared with a national average of about $ 217 in the same year. The two estimates indicate a decrease in the ratio between average income in agriculture and the national average from about 77% to 55% between 1956 and 1965.

Among the urban population the most privileged are, of course, the inhabitants of capital cities where most of manufacturing, educational and health services, and the various media of entertainment and culture tend to concentrate and where per capita income could be at least four times the national average.[56]

In view of such a high degree of dualism national averages lose much of their significance and the nation-state becomes highly inadequate as a unit in per capita income comparisons. The fact that the way of life of the nomads of Arabia makes it difficult to estimate their number should not be regarded simply as a problem facing the statistician in his attempt

---

with 25.8% of the urban population (U.A.R.: Central Agency for Public Mobilization and Statistics: *Population Growth and its Challenges to Development*, *op. cit.*, p. 226). For other estimates see Wazzan, *op. cit.*, p. 204; El-Mallakh, R.: *The Economics of Rapid Growth: Libya*, *op. cit.*, p. 313; Hassan, S.: *op. cit.*, p. 246 and U.N.: *Report on the World Social Situation, 1963*, p. 149.

[54] Mabro, R.: *Industrial Growth, Agricultural Under-Employment and the Lewis Model*, *op. cit.*, p. 337.

[55] Clawson & others, *op. cit.*

[56] See Mclouglin, P.: The Sudan's Three Towns: A Demographic and Economic Profile of An African Urban Complex, Part I: Introductory and Demography, *Economic Development and Cultural Change*, Oct. 1963, pp. 75-6 and Part II: *Output and Expenditure*, Jan. 1964, p. 159.

A more recent estimate for Egypt indicates that the governorate with the highest per capita income (Cairo) had an average per capita income during 1964/5-66/7 which was two and a half times that of the lowest (the Borders' Governorates) and that per capita income in the latter was about half the per capita income of the country as a whole. This is to be compared, for example, with a country like Britain where the average income of different areas vary only around 10% of the national average. (See Kheir El-Dine, H.: Some Aspects of Regional Differences in the U.A.R., *L'Égypte Contemporaine*, Jan. 1971, pp. 76-82 and Seers, D. & Joy, L. (eds.): *Development in a Divided World*, Pelican, 1971, p. 15).

at estimating the per capita income of the state of Saudi Arabia, but should rather throw doubt on the value of the whole exercise.

5. *Over-Urbanization*

During the last few decades Arab urban population has been increasing at rates not only higher than the present rate of developed countries but even higher than that experienced by these countries during their periods of fastest urban growth. The Arab population of cities of 100,000 or more inhabitants has been growing at annual rates ranging from 5.2% in Iraq (1947-57) and 6.0% in Syria (1960-68) to over 16% in Kuwait (1961-65) compared with only 1.42% for the U.S.A. (1950-60), 1.8% for Sweden (1950-60) and —3.1% for U.K. (1951-61),[57] and compared with an average rate of increase of total urban population of nine European countries of 2.1% during their periods of fastest urban growth, mostly in the latter half of the 19th century. Even in such countries as the U.S.A., Australia and New Zealand, which received large numbers of immigrants, this rate did not exceed 4.2% per year.[58]

In Arab capital cities the population has been growing at even faster rates (see Table 34). Thus the population of Beirut is estimated to have doubled in 10 years (1954-64), that of Amman increased ninefold in 13 years (1948-61) while every year the population of Cairo increases by more than 100,000 persons.[59]

Table 34

Average Annual Growth Rates of Population of Capital Cities

Capital City	*Period*	%	*Capital City*	*Period*	%
Cairo	60-66	3.9	Baghdad	57-65	8.3
Damascus	60-66	3.9	Riyadh	62-68	10.0
Tripoli	62-64	4.7	Khartoum	63-66	10.8
Amman	61-66	6.1	Kuwait City	61-65	18.0

Source: UNESOB: *Studies on Selected Development Problems in Various Countries in the Middle East*, 1970, p. 76.

[57] U.N.: *Urbanization. Development Policies and Planning*, International Development Review, No. 1, N.Y., 1968, p. 81 and *Demographic Yearbooks.*

[58] Davis, K.: The Urbanization of the Human Population, in Breese, G. (ed.): *The City in Newly Developing Countries*, Princeton University, 1969, p. 15.

[59] Hurwitz, J.: *The Politics of Rapid Population Growth*, *op. cit.*, p. 93; Remba, *op. cit.*, p. 64.

But it is not only with regard to the increase in the urban population that the Arab world is showing such high rates, but also with regard to the rate of urbanization, i.e. the rate of increase in the proportion of urban to total population. In 1801, not more than about one tenth of the population of England and Wales was living in cities of 100,000 or more and it took no less than 40 years for this proportion to double.[60] In contrast, a similar increase in the proportion of the population living in urban areas took no more than 10 years in Libya and even less in Iraq.[61] Thus, while in England and Wales, the urban population did not exceed 20% until the "industrial revolution" was virtually completed, by the mid-1960's this proportion had already been exceeded in all the nine Arab countries with the exception only of the Sudan and Saudi Arabia (see Table 35).

Table 35

Total and Urban Population

Country	*Year*	*Total Population*	*Urban Population*	*% of Urban to Total Population*
Kuwait	1965	467,333	373,871	80.0
Lebanon	1964	2,246,000	1,020,611 [a]	45.4 [a]
Iraq	1965	8,047,415	3,548,910	44.1
Jordan	1966	2,100,801	907,280	43.2
Egypt	1966	30,076,000	11,970,000	39.8
Syria	1966	5,450,994	2,038,672	37.4
Libya	1964	1,564,000	385,000	24.6
Saudi Arabia	1968	4,861,206	999,464	20.6
Sudan	1966	13,700,000	—	—

[a] Inhabitants of Beirut and Tripol only.
(—) Not available.

Source: Taken or calculated from UNESOB: *Studies on Selected Development Problems*, 1970, p. 76 and the Egyptian Dept. for Statistics and Census: *Annual Book of General Statistics* (1952-67), p. 7.

In five out of the nine Arab countries the urban population, in the mid-1960's was no less than 40%. This proportion of urban population was not reached by Japan until the mid-20th century, but Japan's rate of urbanization has been one of the highest in history. In fact, Arab

[60] Davis, *op. cit.*, p. 10. The corresponding proportion for Europe as a whole was only 2.2% in 1800.

[61] In Libya, this proportion rose from 11.9% in 1954 to 22.5% in 1964, and Iraq from 18.8% in 1957 to 40.4% in 1965.

countries are not only more urbanized now than most underdeveloped countries, but some of them have a proportion of population in large cities (of 100,000 or more inhabitants) which is very close to or higher than the average proportion of some of the economically advanced regions.[62]

In an unpublished lecture delivered in 1954, R. Parke, Jr. suggested that Egypt was an "overurbanized" country.[63] He pointed out how, in 1947, Egypt already had a proportion of its population living in cities of 100,000 or more inhabitants, greater than that of Sweden or France, and that this degree of urbanization was far greater than Egypt's degree of economic development would lead us to expect. A few years later, Professor B. Hoselitz [64] made the same suggestion, this time for underdeveloped countries generally. He pointed out that in Asia "although the proportion of urban population is only 13%, the proportion of non-agricultural labour is roughly 30%. However, at a similar degree of urbanization in the Western countries, the U.S. (1850's), France (1860's), Germany (1880's) and Canada (1890's) had roughly 55% of their labour force engaged in non-agricultural occupations." [65] In this sense, then, overurbanization is taken to mean that "at comparable levels of urbanization the developed countries of today had a correspondingly greater proportion of their labour force engaged in non-agricultural occupations." [66]

In this sense most of the nine Arab countries could be described as overurbanized, if one is to compare the proportions of their urban populations (Table 35) with the proportions of their populations engaged in non-agricultural activity (Table 33). The only exceptions would be Kuwait, owing to her unusually low agricultural population, and possibly the Sudan, whose data is not available.

The very concept of overurbanization has come under heavy attack, however. One writer criticized it for being based on a comparison with the pattern of urbanization that took place in the now-developed countries while there is no reason to believe that if a country does not conform

[62] See E.C.A.: *Size and Growth of Urban Population in Africa,* in Breese, *op. cit.*, p. 131.

[63] A paper read at the annual meeting of the Eastern Sociological Society, April 3, 1954. See Davis, K. and Golden, H.: Urbanization and the Development of Pre-Industrial Areas, in *Economic Development and Cultural Change*, Oct. 1954, pp. 6-24.

[64] Hoselitz, B., Urbanization and Economic Growth in Asia, *Economic Development and Cultural Change*, Oct., 1957, pp. 45-54.

[65] *Ibid.*, pp. 226-8.

[66] Joint U.N./UNESCO: *Seminar Report on Urbanization in Asia and the Far East*, Bangkok, 1956, quoted in Sovani, N.: *The Analysis of Overurbanization*, published in Breese (ed.), *op. cit.*, p. 322.

to that particular pattern, it is to be classed as abnormal.[67] Others have rejected the suggestion that overurbanization exists on the sole ground that they have found a strong correlation between per capita income and urbanization, even among the underdeveloped countries. According to them "this suggests that the drive to urbanization in underdeveloped countries, if it did exist, would not be as damaging as the overurbanization thesis suggests, for per capita income levels and urbanization are positively and closely related in such countries." [68] Still another writer considers that what is more critical than the problem of overurbanization, at least in Egypt, is that of over-concentration of the urban population in relatively few cities. According to her "*the mass movement* to the cities (in Egypt) *may be premature* but it *is* none the less *both inevitable and necessary* . . . Egypt has no choice but to industrialize and urbanize." She asserts that "what overurbanization there is presents no threat to economic or cultural development, nor is it likely to prove more than temporary." [69]

None of these criticisms, however, seem powerful enough to lead us to reject such a suggestive concept as overurbanization. Correlations between per capita income and urbanization, however high, do not provide a good enough basis for dismissing overurbanization as nonexistent. It may very well be that the same factors that inflate per capita income, such as, say, the growth of government administration or the army, may also tend to foster the rapid growth of cities. It is possible, however, that rapid urbanization may in these cases do more harm to economic development than good. Per capita income may have risen even faster and development may have been more balanced and less precarious with less rapid urbanization.

Similarly, given the present rates of industrialization in the Arab world there is nothing "inevitable" or "necessary" about such a rate of mass movement to the cities. It is true that Arab countries are underindustrialized but, given their present level of industrialization, they are also

---

[67] Sovani, *op. cit.*, p. 305.

[68] Kamershen, D., Further Analysis of Over-urbanization, *Economic Development and Cultural Change*, Jan. 1969, p. 240.

[69] Abu-Lughod, J.: Urbanization in Egypt, Present State and Future Prospects, *Economic Development and Cultural Change*, April, 1965, p. 315. The emphasis is hers. See also Murphey, R.: *Urbanization in Asia*, in Breese (ed.), *op. cit.*, p. 65 where he states that "Less urbanization would probably be worse than more, either as a symptom of lesser vigor in the economy or as a cause. It is, after all in cities that economic growth concentrates, especially of the kind which Asia is currently seeking: industrialization."

overurbanized. Cairo may have more than its due share of the urban population but it also has more than its due share of the total population. Arab capital cities have not only got more than their due share of manufacturing and productive investment but they have also grown far beyond their own productive capacity. Nor is there any good reason to believe that it is overconcentration rather than overurbanization which is the "more critical" problem. It is at least as plausible to argue that problems that arise out of parasitic growth are more serious than those arising simply out of a geographical misallocation of investment.

It is perfectly correct to refuse to use the term overurbanization merely on the ground that a country has been urbanized faster than the western countries. We may only use this comparison as a warning against treating more urbanization as a necessarily favourable phenomenon. But we do not need to fall back on such a comparison to justify the description of present Arab countries as overurbanized. The term can still be aptly used to convey the idea that urbanization in the Arab world has been largely dissociated from the growth of manufacturing, or that its present pattern has some detrimental effects on economic development.

We have already seen how manufacturing still makes a very modest contribution to total employment in all the Arab countries,[70] but what is more relevant to the present thesis, is the modest *growth* of production and employment in manufacturing compared with the growth of urban population. In Egypt the proportion of urban population increased, between 1947 and 1960 from 33% to 37%. During the same period the share of industry in the total labour force increased much less rapidly, from 12.3% to 12.6%.[71] In a period of 11 years (1952-63) the growth of Egyptian industry did not create new employment opportunities for more than 350,000 persons, meanwhile the population of Cairo alone was increasing by more than this every three years. Similarly, in Syria, the proportion of the population residing in cities of 100,000 or more, increased from 26.4% to 31.3% between 1960 and 1968. During the same period the proportion of the economically active population in manufacturing hardly increased at all. In Iraq, the proportion of the population of cities of 100,000 or more increased from 18.8% to 40.4% between 1957 and 1965 while the share of manufacturing industry in the GDP remained more or less constant at around 9%.

In order to explain the higher rates of Arab urban growth when com-

[70] See Chapter I, Section 3.

[71] U.A.R.: Central Agency for Public Mobilization and Statistics: *Population Growth in the U.A.R. and its Challenges to Development*, (Arabic), 1966, p. 115.

pared with the earlier urbanization of the West, one should, therefore, look for factors that must have been more powerful than the growth of manufacturing.

One group of factors is demographic. First, there is the higher natural rate of population growth in the country as a whole which is reflected in a higher rate of growth in urban as well as rural areas. Secondly, the present death rates in Arab cities are distinctly lower than those in the countryside owing to better sanitary conditions in the city. This is in sharp contrast to the situation in Western cities during the industrial revolution when poorer health conditions and more frequent epidemics in the cities often made their death rates higher than in the countryside.[72] Thirdly, a much earlier and greater difference between urban and rural birth rates was present in the now-advanced countries. While as early as 1800 urban women in U.S.A. already had 36% fewer children than rural women did,[73] no significant difference has yet been reported between Arab city and country birth rates.

These last two factors: a lower death rate in the city, and a smaller difference between city and country birth rates explain why the present rapid increase in urbanization in the Arab world is less dependent on rural-urban migration than that experienced in the last century. This does not mean, however, that migration is not an important factor. For most of the nine Arab capital cities the annual rate of population growth is more than double that of the natural rate. In Baghdad, Beirut and Cairo, the proportion of village migrants to the total population of the city ranges between one fourth and one third of its total population and, at least in Cairo, this proportion is rising.[74] Similarly, according to the first population census of the Sudan, the natural rate of increase of population of the Three Towns was 2.4% annually, while the rate of increase due to local migration was 2.5%.[75]

[72] In 1841, the expectation of life for England and Wales as a whole was 41 years compared with 36 for London and 26 for Liverpool and Manchester. Higher city death rates continued in England as late as the period 1901-10. (See Davis, *op. cit.*, p. 12).

[73] *Ibid.*, pp. 12-3.

[74] See Gulick, J.: Village and City: Cultural Continuities in Twentieth Century Middle Eastern Cultures, in: Lapidus, I. (ed.): *Middle Eastern Cities*, University of California Press, Berkley, 1969, pp. 122-153; Abu-Lughod, J.: *Migrant Adjustment to City Life: The Egyptian Case*, in: Breese (ed.), *op. cit.*, p. 378 and Abu-Lughod, J.: *Varieties of Urban Experience: Contrast, Coexistence and Coalescence in Cairo*, in: Lapidus, I., *op. cit.*, pp. 168-9. In 1957 no less than 57% of industrial workers in Baghdad were rural migrants.

[75] See Mazari, S.: Greater Khartoum, in Berger, M. (ed.): *The New Metropolis in the Arab World*, Allen and Unwin, London, 1963, p. 122. According to the U.N. *1970*

Differences between rural-urban migration in underdeveloped countries today and that which occurred earlier in the now-developed countries are usually stated in terms of a contrast between the "push" and "pull" factors. For, while in the earlier experience rural migrants were mainly attracted by the increasing employment opportunities in the towns, the urbanization of the underdeveloped countries today is activated mainly by the deteriorating conditions in rural areas. In Arab countries a variety of factors have in fact been working on both sides. On the "push" side there was the sluggish increase in agricultural output, but there was also the two wars with Israel of 1948 and 1967 which drove Palestinian refugees mainly to Jordanian towns. It is also worth noting that the rural migrants of the last century in the West were also pushed off the land, although in this case agricultural labour was made redundant not merely by the increase in the population/land ratio but also by the rapid technological progress in agriculture. This last difference, coupled with the difference in the natural rates of population growth help to explain the important fact that while Arab urbanization has not been accompanied by an *absolute* decline in the rural population, in the earlier experience rural population declined both absolutely and relatively to total population. On the "pull" side there has been, in the Arab case, the rapid increase in oil production which contributed to rapid urbanization both in the oil countries and in Lebanon, not so much as a source of employment but rather by the rapid growth of services and of building industries. There was also the attraction created by the rapid growth of the government sector. Much more powerful than industrial employment as a motive for Arab rural-urban migration has been the urge to become a government employee, to join the army or the university, or simply the "psychic" as opposed to the economic attraction of the city.[76]

6. *Income Inequalities and Economic Development*

One reason for the neglect of the problem of income-distribution in underdeveloped countries is of course their poverty.[77] In the words of T. Morgan:

Report on the World Social Situation, 50% of the growth of Amman's population as well as most of the growth of the seven major cities in Saudi Arabia have been due to in-migration (p. 81).

[76] According to Janet Abu-Lughod, "many a villager now in Cairo opted for urban life after an army discharge, having received some education and training in service which equipped him for opportunities most available in the metropolis". (*Varieties of Urban Experience*, *op. cit.*, p. 171). In the Sudan many rural migrants are attracted to Omdurman for religious reasons, being the capital of Al-Mahdi.

[77] Another reason is what Myrdal calls "scientific diplomacy" or the art of avoiding

> "Where nearly all people are very poor the sentiment for reducing a wide range of above-average but still moderate income-groups to plainly less than adequate consumption can hardly be strong." [78]

This is obviously inapplicable to Kuwait, for whom growth rather than distribution should be considered a marginal problem. Its significance may also be doubtful for Libya or Lebanon where per capita income is considerably higher than in most other underdeveloped countries. But even for other Arab countries where per capita income is much lower, the argument seems to gain in strength only in so far as the standard of comparison is the income levels of advanced countries. The fact that a perfectly equal distribution of Iraq's national income, for example, would not give each person more than about one seventeenth of U.S. per capita income may not give a sufficient cause for excitement over equality. If the aim, however, is to eradicate the worst forms of "absolute" poverty and to meet the much simpler demands of the poorest sections of the population, a great deal seems to be possible through redistribution. It would emerge, for example, that if the average income of the richest 5% of the population of Iraq is reduced to half its 1960 level, the other half being transferred to the poorest 20%, the average income of the latter would be multiplied more than 9 times.

But even if the economist was ready to admit that the immediate effects of redistribution on welfare may not be insignificant he may still fear that it may have negative effects on growth. This fear is largely the result of reading the last-century experience of the now-developed countries where inequality seems to have been favourable or at least not a serious obstacle to their rapid growth. But contemporary conditins in the Arab world are so different that a case, at least equally as strong can be made for the favourable effects of greater equality on economic development.

Compared with the puritanical upper-income groups of the last century in the West and the strong drive for rapid capital accumulation shown by the Soviet state in this century, the Arab upper-classes as well as the new military elites show much lower propensities to save and invest in socially productive channels. It is through this small section of the population, but particularly through the new bureaucratic elites, that the international demonstration effect makes for a high propensity

---

a subject that must ultimately lead to a discussion of political power and corruption. (*The Challenge of World Poverty*, *op. cit.*, p. 119 & 237).

[78] Distribution of Income in Developed and Underdeveloped Countries, *Economic Journal*, 1956, p. 161.

to consume for the country as a whole. These new elites are likely to appear to the lower-income groups as more imitatable than their predecessors whose social distinction rested on more than mere wealth. They also seem more inclined to display their newly acquired wealth than both the superseded landlords, who tended to enjoy it in the privacy of walled-in palaces, or the rich of the developed countries who keep most of their wealth in the form of stocks and bonds.

In countries where so much depends on the government official taking the right decision with regard to public investment and on the readiness of even the poorest sections of the population to accept restraints on consumption, economic development must suffer from a system of distribution in which the wrong decision is often more highly rewarded, in which the lower strata of the government bureaucracy are discouraged by comparing the high salaries at the top with their own poor pay and with their governments' socialist slogans, and where petty bribes are accepted as a desperate measure for a redistribution of income which the government has failed to enforce.

The favourable effects of inflation in so far as its redistributes income in favour of a class characterized by a high propensity to save and invest are largely lost when home industries are insufficiently protected, as is the case of the oil countries and Lebanon, and when the beneficiaries of inflation are mainly the traders and speculators.

The Classical economists' argument that a more equal distribution would merely lead to faster population growth, thus wiping out whatever benefit the poor may have reaped, is much less relevant to underdeveloped countries of today where population growth is much less the result of increasing income than of modern medicine. On the other hand, a wider market brought about by greater equality was probably less vital to Europe in its early stages of growth than it is to underdeveloped countries today with their per capita income being lower than that of the presently developed countries before their initial phases of industrialization [79] and with the all too-familiar problems facing their exports.

Inequality of opportunities in education also seem more detrimental to growth in present-day underdeveloped countries than at earlier times when industries were able to make more use of traditional craft skills and when entrepreneurs as well as labourers drew more upon traditional skills and inventiveness and relied more on education through

---

[79] See Kuznets, S.: Economic Growth and Income Inequality, *American Economic Review*, 1955, p. 25.

the family or personal apprenticeship than upon formal education.[80]

Finally, there are good reasons to believe that while the process of urbanization in the West seems to have generated values and attitudes that were favourable to economic development, the wide gap between the levels of income and ways of life *within* Arab cities tend to obstruct the development of these values.

On their arrival to the city few rural migrants find employment in industry and most of the rest become petty traders, porters, peddlars or are charitably employed as office servants. But it is precisely because of this failure of Arab cities to absorb rural migrants in productive occupations that the rapid urbanization of the Arab world is not likely to prove as favourable to economic development.

So many of the urban values which are favourable to growth are dependent upon the success of the rural migrant in securing a more or less permanent source of income. Failing this, the rural migrant is likely to delay the severance of his ties with the village and to continue to rely on traditional sources of security provided by his family or tribe. Lacking a stable city life, the rural migrant is forced to keep his ties with his rural kin alive by his frequent and regular returns to the village and by being ready to receive frequent visits in return. The persistence of this kind of interdependence, financial as well as emotional, tends to encourage rural migrants on arriving in the city, to settle in clusters of their own which, in their turn, help to perpetuate their village customs and to strengthen their resistance to the urban way of life.[81]

---

[80] On this point see Fallers, L.: Equality, Modernity and Democracy in the New States, in Geertz, C. (ed.): *Old Societies and New States*, The Free Press of Glencoe, London, 1963, p. 191.

[81] There is hardly any Arab capital city in which inhabitants of slums do not constitute a sizeable proportion of its population. This is true of Amman and Damascus as it is true of Beirut where slums inhabited by rural migrants as well as by refugees have now been in existence for over forty years. In Cairo some 30% of the population in the early 1960's were classified as living in slums of which some have a density of 12 persons or more per room. The two densest slums in Cairo, Boulaq and Bab-al-Shaariya, which are very close to the central business district, have densities of up to 900,000 persons per square mile. (See Abu-Lughod, J.: *Migrant Adjustment to City Life*, *op. cit.*, p. 126). But "shanty towns" are probably no more conspicuous as in Baghdad where the famous *sarifas* account for about 45% of the housing of the entire city. In view of Iraq's vast possibilities for agricultural expansion, Arnold Toynbee has described Baghdad's *sarifas* as "the most irrational example (of rural-urban migration) that I have seen at first hand." (*Cities on the Move*, Oxford University Press, 1970, pp. 209-10). One example of the prestige attached to the subject of economic growth compared with that of the direct impact of poverty is provided by a recent U.N. report on the Arab urban environment in which the author does not forget to mention that "slums are an environmental problem also in so far as they are an un-

With a relatively low rate of increase in employment and with prohibitive rents, young married couples often continue to share their parents' house or, alternatively, older people may move to live with their married children. For example, it has been found that the Muslim households of Amman and of Tripoli (Lebanon), averaging 7.0 and 6.7 persons respectively, are essentially of the same size as those in the villages.[82] According to one writer, rural migrants to Cairo often inhabit districts which are close to the bus terminals leading to their village and where "interior streets and alleyways are seldom used for wheeled traffic, leaving undisturbed the rural functions of the street as pathway, meeting place, playground and tethering area for animals." [83] In Baghdad, rural migrants built their *sarifas* so that members of each tribal group were clustered together and their shaykhs continued to exercise their authority, settling disputes and maintaining guesthouses.[84]

When there are relatively few opportunities for work in the towns and when employment is less permanent and less secure, women and children are often left behind in the village. But even when women and children do accompany the men to the city, they are likely to find that employment opportunities for them are even more scarce than for their men.[85] The "liberating" function of the city is therefore to that extent weakened. In fact, in certain sections of the city, women may become more severely segregated than they were in the village because of the greater likelihood of encounters with strangers. More important perhaps is the fact that, with such a pattern of urbanization, the fertility rate may not show any significant decline with the growth of towns. This is due not only to the difficulty of securing employment for women but also to the fact that

---

economic use of scarce land since they are usually one-storey shacks." But forgetting that slum dwellers are either unemployed or underemployed, the report goes on to say that "when there is no running water, it is time-consuming to clean food, to clean the house..." (UNESOB: *Environmental Implications of Urban Settlements* (mimeo.), 1971, p. 27).

[82] Gulick, *op. cit.*, p. 134. In the Three Towns of the Sudan, the average number of families per house was found to be 1.4 (Al-Mazari, *op. cit.*, p. 125).

[83] Abu-Lughod, J.: *Migrant Adjustment to City Life*, *op. cit.*, p. 383. The same writer observes that "many an Egyptian coffee shop is run by a villager to serve men from that particular village. News of the village is exchanged, mutual assistance for employment is given and the venture more resembles a closed club than a commercial enterprise" (*ibid.*, p. 387).

[84] Gulick, *op. cit.*, p. 149. The same phenomenon is observed for Tripoli (Lebanon).

[85] In the Baghdad area for example, the 1954 census showed that female employment constituted no more than 3.3% of total employment and fell to 2.5% in the larger establishments. (See Al-Madfai, K.: Baghdad, in: Berger, M.: *The New Metropolis in the Arab World*, *op. cit.*, p. 52).

with persistently low incomes, the engagement of children in petty services may also persist and economic ambition would be considerably reduced. With low incomes and little security parents may continue to regard their children, as they did in the village, as the most reliable source of security in their old age. All of these factors combine to make the larger family much less un-attractive. In fact, in certain areas of Cairo comprising some 14% of Cairo's population, fertility rates were found to be higher than in the village.[86] Similarly, in the Baghdad area, the average size of families was shown, by the 1959 census, to be 6.16 persons per family compared with a national average of 5.65.[87]

Professor Hoselitz rightly remarks that: "If progress towards universalistic achievement-oriented social values have been difficult in the cities of Asia and Africa, it is not due to the stubbornness of the people or their 'superstitous' adherence to old ways of life, but rather to the very unfavourable conditions under which they have been brought to the city and under which they continue to exist." [88]

Nor is the assimilation of the rural migrants by the urban way of life merely a matter of time. It is an oversimplification to dismiss this persistence of rural characteristics in Arab cities simply by saying that these cities have not yet become "truly urban". The desired assimilation depends not only on time but also on the nature of urbanization itself. Hence, Arab cities may not simply be in a stage of transition to the western model of city life but rather exhibiting peculiar features of their own. These features may very well continue to exist so long as this pattern of urbanization persists.

In fact, the very high rate of urbanization in the Arab world may itself obstruct the process of development. It is customary to think of the city as assimilating the rural migrants; but this may be true only up to a certain level of migration rates. If the rate of migration exceeds this level one may more aptly describe the process as one of "invasion". Far from being assimilated, the rural migrants may actually come to dominate the city, their way of life becoming paramount and with the city's cultural and political life merely trying to accommodate to their taste.

Turning to the other side of the rural-urban relationship, it should not be surprising to find that with this pattern of urbanization, the villagers have little to gain from the rapid growth of cities. This is not simply

[86] Abu-Lughod, J.: *Varieties of Urban Experience*, *op. cit.*, p. 177.

[87] Al-Madfai, *op. cit.*, p. 51.

[88] Hoselitz, B.: The City, The Factory and Economic Growth, *American Economic Review, Papers and Proceedings*, 1955, p. 179.

because the city produces little of what the peasants might need. With an increasing gap between city and country the city looks increasingly outward in search not only for luxury consumer goods, but also for food, raw materials and markets. This is all the more true the more sluggish is the increase in agricultural productivity, the greater the flow of foreign aid, particularly in the form of food, the more liberal is the country's importation policy and the more unequal the distribution of income. Home-produced consumption goods become inadequate for the taste of town-dwellers, as can be clearly seen in Lebanon,[89] and the rural inhabitants grow increasingly unable to purchase the products of domestic industries where wages are governed more by political than by economic factors, and where the products themselves are affected by expensive foreign tastes.

Nor do Arab cities show greater ability as exporters of culture. This is again partly due to the wide gap between city and country which tends to make professionals resist moving to the villages. But it is also due to the over-concentration of the urban population in the capital cities.[90] As Professor Issawi puts it:

> "The 'demonstration effect' of a given amount of modern culture concentrated in the metropolis is presumably much smaller than that of an equal amount divided among, say, half a dozen provincial towns, which could make an impact on a much wider surrounding population." [91]

Thus, in this as in many other respects, Arab countries seem to be having the worst of two worlds. For while the role of Arab capital cities as outlets of economic progress to the wider countryside is reduced by over-concentration, they are themselves widely open to the demonstration effect of western consumption levels.

[89] In *Lebanon* the value of imports of consumer durables (radios, T.V. sets, washing machines, refrigerators and private cars) during 1969 (excluding re-exports, customs and other duties) was five times its level in 1951, compared with an increase of 230% in the value of all imports during the same period. Between 1951 and 1967 the number of private cars in Lebanon increased at two and a half times the rate of increase in the number of cars and buses used for public transport. Similarly, in *Syria* the number of private cars increased almost tenfold between 1947 and 1960 compared with about 50% increase in the number of vehicles used in public transport. In *Egypt* the annual number of imported private cars increased by 228% between 1966 and 1969 and in *Libya* their number in the Western provinces was increasing at the rate of 1000 every month, which is double the rate of 1963. (Beydoun, *op. cit.*, pp. 128-34 & 195; Hilan, *op. cit.*, p. 232; El-Said, *op. cit.*, p. 70 and Farley, *op. cit.*, p. 230).

[90] In no one of the nine Arab countries is the population of the capital city less than 30% of total urban population and the proportion is as high as 46% in Baghdad and 80% in Kuwait (1965).

[91] *Economic Change and Urbanization in the Middle East*, in Lapidus, *op. cit.*, pp. 316-7.

CONCLUSION

1

It is indeed remarkable how Arab countries, starting from such different points and following such different routes have reached such similar results. With or without land reform, the landlords and tribal chiefs have been largely deprived of political power but the agricultural population continues to be discriminated against. With or without socialist slogans, the public sector is growing but the rate of saving is not. The domination of the traditional forms of foreign economic interests has either vanished or is on the decline, even in oil, but is rapidly being replaced by that of a new native class. Rich or poor in agricultural resources, all of them, except Syria, have a growing food deficit, and Syria's surplus is declining. They all have plans and have been investing much higher rates than Europe ever did during the last century and have been urbanizing much faster without making, except for Egypt, any significant change in economic structure. They have received vast funds from foreign governments or companies of which they, without exception, have managed to waste considerable portions and in almost all, the government has been more wasteful than the public.

The one feature which is most generally admitted to be common to all: their common desire to achieve rapid economic development and the pressure of the so-called "revolution of rising expectations" seems, however, to be the one feature most in need of qualification.

A revolution of rising expectation, does undoubtedly exist, but it is by no means that of the large majority of population whose aspirations rarely extend beyond the demand for clean drinking water and slightly more adequate diet and shelter. Those whose expectations are continuously rising, but never satisfied, constitute only a small minority of the urban dwellers whose political influence is strong enough to allow them to hope, not unrealistically, for still higher levels of living.

Rather than showing a general desire for rapid economic development, Arab governments show a surprisingly weak will to achieve it. This is rather the wish of charitable foreign observers who, for a variety of reasons, seem to find it convenient to take Arab governments' expressed wishes at their face value. A much more powerful motive than economic development is the motive to remain in power. This, of course, is neither peculiar to Arab governments nor indeed to the governments of underdeveloped countries. Nor is it necessarily undesirable, except in cases where the desire to perpetuate power comes in direct conflict with the requirements of progress. Among the nine Arab countries, the coinciding of the two motives seem to have come nearest and lasted the longest in Egypt. It is not surprising, therefore, that Egypt was the most successful among them in changing the economic structure, in diversifying exports and in implementing land reform and where planning and the call for Arab integration were taken most seriously. Much more confident in the stability of his regime and subjected to a much stronger pressure from domestic economic problems, but above all, presented with a particularly favourable international climate, Nasser was exceptionally fortunate to find the road to high political stature and power largely coinciding with that of manipulating international politics to his country's own advantage. As soon as the two roads parted, however, little hesitation was shown as to which one to chose. As a result, Egypt witnessed a serious economic setback which started well before the 1967 war.[1]

While in his days of maximum power and popularity Nasser used to ask for people's loyalty to their homeland, in his decline loyalty came to be asked for the revolution, and the country's history was considered to start from the day the revolution started. Egypt continued to be deprived of her own name even after the dissolution of her union with Syria, while the date of the union continues to be a holiday that nobody celebrates. In contrast to its early optimism with regard to the population problem, the Egyptian government made frequent use of it since the early 1960's as the main cause of the country's economic difficulties. Rather than treating the high birth rate as something which Egypt has to learn to live with for a long time, just as, for instance, her poverty in

[1] In an attempt made by I. Adelman and C. Morris to gain insight into the relationship of various social, economic and political factors with the level and pace of development, 74 underdeveloped countries, in which seven of our nine Arab countries were included, were classified with regard to 41 such variables. One of the political variables was "the extent of leadership commitment to economic development," as could be judged mainly by the attitudes of leadership groups and "the extent of their willingness to make purposive attempts to achieve institutional change." The period of which the study was made was 1957-62. Four of the seven Arab countries included in the analysis (Iraq, Lebanon, Libya and Syria) were described as "countries in which there was little or no evidence of leadership commitment to economic development." Jordan and the Sudan were described as countries where "government attempts to alter institutional arrangements unfavourable to economic growth were infrequent or poorly sustained." Only Egypt of the seven countries was regarded as a country "in which government leadership exhibited sustained and reasonably effective commitment to economic development." (*Society, Politics and Economic Development: A Quantitative Approach*, Johns Hopkins, London, 1971, pp. 78-81).

minerals is taken for granted, the Egyptian government, like the Pearson Commission, persists in considering it as the most serious obstacle to development compared with which "no other phenomenon casts a darker shadow." A similar tendency was shown 150 years ago by economists who frequently quoted Malthus in blaming poverty on the poor themselves for breeding too fast. But while the earlier emphasis on the population problem helped to divert attention from the fast increasing profits, the present emphasis helps only to divert the attention from the wastes of government expenditure. The high rate of population growth in Egypt was in fact neither the main factor behind the rapid growth of consumption, nor the easiest problem to solve in a few years. It neither prevented Egypt from achieving a remarkable rate of growth between 1956 and '63 nor was it responsible for the government's spending about one fifth of GDP on the armed forces, nor for a large part of the increase in other items of public consumption. Nor could the obstinacy of Egypt's high birth rate be simply blamed on the persistence of irrational or short-sighted social or religious attitudes. When the existing system of social insurance is so deficient, the only safeguard against deprivation in old-age is to have as many adult children as possible. The provision of a more adequate system of social insurance may still not bring quick results, but it is likely to be much more effective in reducing birth rates than a free distribution of contraceptives.

2

Observing the growing role of Arab governments in the economic and social life of their countries, Charles Issawi remarked that:

> "Sir William Harcourt's statement made nearly seventy years ago 'we are all socialists now' applies to the Middle East of today." [2]

A more apt description of Arab governments is that they have all become "modernizers". The features which they have in common have led not so much to the reduction of poverty as to its modernization, to the creation of a façade of modernity behind which the majority of the population continues to lead virtually the same way of life. It is this function of Arab governments as mediators between their own people and European civilization, whether of the Western or Eastern subvariety, or rather as agents transmitting to their countries only the most superficial aspects of this civilization, not the realization of socialism or economic advance, which could explain the largest number of features

[2] *Economic History of the Middle East*, p. 511.

which they have in common. Only thus can one understand, for instance, their premature adoption of comprehensive planning, their formation of an ineffective Arab common market, their educational imbalances, the over-concentration of services in the capital cities, their invariable preference for capital intensive techniques, their neglect of agriculture and above all, their handing out of the most modern armaments to illiterate and illfed soldiers, which merely resulted in a very short war and a defeat. It is also in this light that one should probably look at such events as the replacement of King Saud by the "more modern" King Faisal before the former King's death, or the more important Yemen campaign of Egypt. In the short-run, this might appear as no more than a frivolous adventure, but in the longer run it may prove to have been the beginning of modernization in the Yemen in which Nasser was playing what is considered by many people's standards a "useful" role. The same may also be true of Libya's 1969 revolution and the severe attacks on moslem orthodoxy in the Sudan as well as in Egypt.

It is indeed in this light that one should consider the whole trend towards the replacement of the land-based elites by army officers and of parliamentary by totalitarian regimes. Probably no other section of the Arab population was more suited to perform this peculiar form of modernization than Arab army officers, with their longer exposure to the West, their fascination by modern western equipment and their keenness on quick results.

Totalitarianism also seems to be a favourable though not a necessary condition for the performance of this task. E. Hoffer writes:

> "Conditions which are optimal for origination are not necessarily optimal for imitation. Origination requires a more or less loose social order in which the individual has leeway to tinker, follow his hunches, and run risks on his own. On the other hand, rapid imitation is facilitated by social compactness, regimentation and concerted action. The individual who is a member of a compact group is more imitative than the individual who is on his own. The unified individual is without a distinct self and, like the child, his mind is without guards against the intrusion of influences from without." [3]

---

[3] *The Ordeal of Change*, pp. 25-6. In the same book we can find a psychological explanation, though an insufficient one, for the tendency of Arab revolutionary leaders to declare themselves enemies of the West and to be among the West's most bitter critics: "the sense of inferiority inherent in the act of imitation breeds resentment ... Now and then in history ... the imitators began by destroying the model and then proceeded to imitate it. We are apparently most at ease when we imitate a defeated or dead model." (p. 22).

Also favourable to the task of creating a façade of modernity, though not so favourable to the reduction of poverty, is the ceaseless emphasis, for which western economists are no less responsible, on the need to close the gap between per capita incomes in the Arab world and those of the advanced countries, a gap which is not only impossible to close for many decades but would perhaps be smaller the less is said about it. Rather than defining a threshold income which every Arab country could determine for itself as a possible target to reach within a relatively short period of time, those who raise the slogan try instead to engage the whole population in a desperate race from which only a few can reap any benefit. A strong desire of a small minority to catch up with western ways of life was thus translated into the desire of the whole population, the majority of whom are either completely unaware of the existence of such a "gap" or, because of their much simpler needs, would find its existence completely irrelevant.

3

Economists have gradually come to realize that economic development is much more tolerant of cultural and institutional variety than they tended to think when they first showed interest in the problems of underdeveloped countries and had less direct experience of their societies and cultures. Neither a strong religious belief, for example, nor an extended family system, nor even the inferior position of women seem necessarily to constitute obstacles to rapid economic advance. Attempts at making a country look more modern do not, however, show the same degree of tolerance. Traditional institutions which are obviously harmless but give the contemporary Arab a sense of identity and self-esteem are, therefore, undermined merely because of their conflict with modernity. Thus the colourful Arab feasts accompanying birth, circumcision, marriage and death are regarded as "backward" and the social pleasure of the month of fasting are kept alive only by the "primitive" poor.

Traditional Arab forms whether in music, dress, furniture or architecture are indiscriminately replaced by western forms. Thus the "revival" of Arab music takes the form of multiplying the number of instruments and dressing the musicians in dinner jackets while "modern architecture (is) used uniformly and indistinguishably from the almost alpine climate of the Lebanese mountain village, to the almost oven-like climate of Kuwait."[4] Just as Egypt's Al-Azhar was modernized so was the pilgrimage

---

[4] Shiber, S.: *Planning Needs and Obstacles,* in: Berger, *op. cit.*, p. 169.

in Arabia.[5] Arab intellectuals, whose knowledge of their countries' intellectual leaders is derived largely from western scholarship, have accepted without questioning the purely western view of regarding as the greatest of these leaders not the most original, scholarly or even influential, but the most eloquent westernizers. A modern Egyptian army officer who, being also a novelist, was appointed as the General Secretary of the Higher Council for the Promotion of Literature, Arts and Social Sciences at one time expressed the view that the insistence on observing strict grammatical rules of Classical Arabic in literature is merely a sign of fastidiousness and that modern ideas were badly in need of the vehicle of the colloquial.

4

It is sad to think that while the gradual loss of cultural differentiation in the advanced countries today, as well as their deteriorating environment, are largely the price of their rapid economic development, the same ills are being suffered by Arab countries for little or no reward.

In the West, as in the Arab countries, the growth of cities was accompanied by the emergence of slums; but while there, investment in working-class houses was sluggish because it had to compete with investment in manufacturing and railways, in the Arab world its sluggishness is largely due to its failure to compete with middle-class housing. Air and water are polluted in Arab cities not so much because of fast industrialization as because of their fast-growing consumption. They are noisy and congested without the country having a car industry. Their architecture is ugly not because the Arabs produce ugly designs but rather because they are demolishing their fine old buildings to import foreign forms. Agricultural land and open grounds are not encroached upon mainly by factories, nor by houses built for industrial labourers but mainly by luxury blocks of flats, grandiose buildings and government offices. Slume are growing not because there is so much expansion in industrial employment but simply because agriculture is neglected.

---

[5] Describing the transformation of the Saudi port of Jedda, Van Der Meulen wrote: "For centuries Jedda's streets had been the first stage of that possibly greatest of all human dramas called the *hajj*, but now a new dawn had appeared. The Holy Land of Islam no longer depended on the income from the *hajj*. How poor was that income now compared with the profit from oil! ... Pilgrims now walk ashore from ships that tie up alongside a modern pier. They then go straight through concrete customs buildings to 'pilgrim town', a practical, ugly, modern kind of pilgrim barracks, and in motor buses they are carried over an asphalt road to Mecca. An ever-growing number of pilgrims arrive by air and touch the sacred soil of Hejaz when they climb down to the concrete runway of an American-built aerodrome. If they arrive at night-time they are greeted by the neon lights and advertisements telling them that Coca-Cola will do them good." (*The Wells of Ibn Saud, op. cit.*, p. 123 & 224-5).

History has known "consumer" as well as "producer" cities. In the former, the inhabitants import most of the goods they need, export relatively little and tend to dominate other cities as well as the countryside either militarily, economically or both.[6] Arab capital cities exhibit this characteristic more strongly than that of a producer city, and this being the case, the conflict between the quality of life and economic development appears to be to a large extent illusory. In order to have capital cities of finer quality, there is no need to slow down industrialization but simply to build more industries in the provinces. To get rid of noise and congestion, there is no need to curb the production of private cars, since the country either does not produce any, or if it does, economic development will often benefit by closing it down or by producing buses instead. Nor does the Arab country need to spend some of its scarce resources on eradicating the slums and building new homes, since rural migration may slow down considerably if only more investment is directed to agriculture.

On the other hand, to realise that it is mainly consumption and not production which is damaging Arab environment should make one much more pessimistic about a possible solution. It is much easier for a highly productive society to adapt its products to the requirements of a higher quality life than it is for a parasitic consumer suffering from a heavy feeling of inferiority which drives him to copy indiscriminately whatever the more advanced countries are doing. Moreover, when the growth of the urban population is relatively independent of the growth of productive capacity, the financial ability of the government and of municipal authorities to improve the conditions of city life is not likely to grow as fast as the city population. Prices of land are likely to soar to levels beyond the reach of a municipality desiring its conversion for public use, as is only too evident in Beirut. Whatever funds might be available for such purposes are likely in any case to be used to the benefit of that portion of the city population which has the greatest political influence. It is also far easier to tax the producer for whatever damage he might do to the environment than to tax the consumer. It is probably also much easier to control private producers *and* consumers than to restrain the bureaucracy which is the one both to draw and to break the plan.

---

[6] On this distinction see, Comhaire, J. and Cahnman, W.: *How Cities Crew*, Madison, N.J., 1962, p. 11; Bocke, J.: *Economics and Economic Policy of Dual Societies as Examplified by Indonesia*, Institute of Pacific Relations, N.Y., 1953 and Viner, J.: America's Aims and the Progress of Underdeveloped Countries, in: Hoselitz, B. (ed.): *The Progress of Underdeveloped Areas*, Chicago, 1952, pp. 192-3.

BIBLIOGRAPHY

Abdel-Khalek, M.: *Agrarian Reform in Egypt:* A Field Study of the Agrarian Reform in Two Typical Areas during the Period 1953-63, unpublished Ph.D. thesis, London University, 1971.

Abdel-Malek, A.: *Egypt: Military Society*, Vintage Books, N.Y., 1968.

Abu-Lughod, J.: Migrant Adjustment to City Life: the Egyptian Case, published in Breese, G. (ed.): *The City in Newly Developing Countries*, Princeton University, 1969.

— —: Urbanization in Egypt: Present State and Future Prospects, *Economic Development and Cultural Change*, April 1965.

Adams, M. (ed.): *The Middle East, A Handbook*, Anthony Blond, London, 1971.

Adelman, I. and C. Morris: *Society, Politics & Economic Development: A Quantitative Approach*, Johns Hopkins, London, 1971.

— —: An Anatomy of Income Distribution in Developing Countries, *Development Digest*, Oct. 1971.

Albino, O.: *The Sudan, A Southern Point of View*, Oxford, 1970.

Al-Dagany, B.: *An Analysis of Some Aspects of Arab Economic Relations*, Institute of Arab Studies, Cairo, 1962. (Arabic)

Al-Galeely, A.: *Population Conditions in Iraq*, Institute of Arab Studies, Cairo, 1969. (Arabic)

Al-Ghandour, A.: *Arab Economic Intergration*, Institute of Arab Studies, Cairo, 1970. (Arabic)

Al-Habeeb, A.: *Lectures on the Development of Iraq's Foreign Trade*, Institute of Arab Studies, Cairo, 1967. (Arabic)

Allan, J.A.: Some Recent Developments in Libyan Agriculture, *Middle East Economic Papers*, 1969.

Alnasrawi, A.: *Financing Economic Development in Iraq*, Praeger, N.Y., 1967.

Al-Said, R.: The Role of the Middle Class in the Egyptian Society, *Al-Taliaa*, March 1972. (Arabic)

Al-Qazzaz, A.: Political Order, Stability and Officers, A Comparative Study of Iraq, Syria and Egypt, *Middle East Forum*, 1969.

Amin, G.: *Food Supply and Economic Development, With Special Reference to Egypt*, Cass, London, 1966

— —: The Role of Natural Resources in Arab Economic Development, *Journal of Legal and Economic Studies*, Ain-Shams University, January 1972. (Arabic)

— —: Some Problems of Labour and Population in the Arab World, *L'Égypte Contemporaine*, April 1971. (Arabic)

Andreski, S.: *Parasitism and Subversion, the Case of Latin America*, Weidenfeld & Nicholson, London, 1966.

— —: *The African Predicament, A Study in the Pathology of Modernization*, Michael Joseph, London, 1969.

Awad, L.: *The University and the New Society*, Al-Dar Al-Kawmeya, Cairo, (not dated, 1965?). (Arabic)

Awad, M. H.: The Evolution of Landownership in the Sudan, *Middle East Journal*, Spring, 1971.

Azhari, N.: *L'Évolution Du Système Économique Libanais*, L.G.D.J., Paris, 1970.

Bank of Sudan: *Annual Reports.*

Baran, P.: *The Political Economy of Growth*, London, 1957.

Bauer, P.: *Dissent on Development*, Weidenfeld & Nicholson, London, 1971.

Berger, M.: *The Arab World Today*, Anchor Books, 1962.

—— (ed.): *The New Metropolis in the Arab World*, Allen & Unwin, London, 1963.

Beydoun, T.: *The Influence of Economic System on Consumer's Behaviour in Lebanon*, Social Science Institute, Lebanese University, Beirut, 1970. (Arabic)

Binder, L. (ed.): *Politics in Lebanon*, J. Wiley, N.Y., 1966.

Boktor, A.: *The Development and Expansion of Education in the U.A.R.*, American University in Cairo Press, Cairo, 1963.

Breese, G. (ed.): *The City in Newly Developing Countries*, Princeton University, 1969

Bullard, R.: *The Middle East, A Political and Economic Survey*, Oxford University Press, 1958.

Clawson, M., H. Landsberg, L. Alexander: *The Agricultural Potential of the Middle East*, American Elsevier Publishing Company, N.Y., 1971.

Cook, M. (ed.): *Studies in the Economic History of the Middle East*, Oxford University Press, London, 1970.

Cooper, Ch. A. and S. Alexander, (eds.): *Economic Development and Population Growth in the Middle East*, American Elsevier, N.Y., 1972.

Copeland, M.: *The Game of Nations*, Weidenfeld & Nicholson, London, 1969.

Corm, G.: *Politique Économique et Planification au Liban, 1953-63*, Librairie de Médicis, Paris, (not dated, 1965?).

Crecelius, D.: Al-Azhar in the Revolution, *Middle East Journal*, Winter 1966.

Davis, K. and H. Colden: Urbanization and the Development of Pre-Industrial Areas, *Economic Development and Cultural Change*, October 1954.

Diab, M.: The First Five-Year Plan of Syria, An Appraisal, *Middle East Economic Papers*, 1960.

——: *Inter-Arab Economic Cooperation, 1951-60*, Economic Research Institute, American University of Beirut, Beirut, 1963.

——: *Environmental Considerations in the Management of Natural Resources in the Middle East*, (mimeo.), UNESOB, Sept. 1971.

Dhahab, S.: *Arab Crude Petroleum*, Institute of Arab Studies, Cairo, 1969. (Arabic)

Dosser, D.: *A Theory of Economic Integration for Developing Countries*, Allen & Unwin, London, 1971.

Economist Intelligence Unit: *Quarterly Economic Review*.

Edens, D. and W. Snavely: Planning and Economic Development in Saudi Arabia, *Middle East Journal*, Winter 1970.

Eid, N.: Merchandise Retailing in Lebanon, *Middle East Economic Papers*, 1969.

El-Mallakh, R.: *Economic Development and Regional Cooperation: Kuwait*, The University of Chicago Press, Chicago, 1968.

——: The Economics of Rapid Growth: Libya, *Middle East Journal*, Summer 1969.

Faculté du Droit et des Sciences Économiques de Grenoble: *Pétrole et Développement Économique Au Moyen-Orient*, Éditions Monton, Paris, 1968.

Farley, R.: *Planning Economic Development in Libya*, Praeger, N.Y., 1972.

Fawzi, S.: *Some Aspects of the Sudanese Economy*, Institute of Arab Studies, Cairo, 1958. (Arabic)

Federation of Arab Chambers of Commerce, Industry and Agriculture: *Arab Economic Development, 1950-65*, Beirut, 1967.

Fisher, S.: *The Middle East*, A History, A. Knope, 1959.

F.A.O.: *Plan Indicatif Mondial pour Le Développement de L'Agriculture, 1965-85*: Proche-Orient, Rome, 1966.

——: *Production Yearbooks.*

Gaitskell, A.: *Gezira: A Story of Development in the Sudan*, Faber & Faber, London, 1959.

Garzouzi, G.: Land Reform in Syria, *Middle East Journal*, Winter-Spring 1963.

Geertz, C. (ed.): *Old Societies and New States*, The Free Press of Glencoe, London, 1963.

Ghattas, E.: Lebanon's Financial Crisis in 1966, A Systemic Approach, *Middle East Journal*, Winter 1971.
Ghoneim, A.: The New Class in Egypt, *Al-Taliaa*, February 1968. (Arabic)
Godfrey, E.: The Brain Drain from Low-Income Countries, *Journal of Development Studies*, April 1970.
Government of Libya: *Statistical Abstract*, 1969.
Grunwald, K. and J. Ronall: *Industrialization in the Middle East*, Council for Middle Eastern Affairs Press, 1966.
Gusten, R.: *Problems of Economic Growth and Planning: the Sudan Example*, Springer-Verlag, Berlin, 1966.
Hamadi, S.: *Towards a Socialist Land Reform*, Beirut, 1964. (Arabic)
Hansen, B.: Distributive Shares in Egyptian Agriculture, *International Economic Review*, 1968.
——: *Economic Development in Syria*, The Rand Corporation, 1969.
——: *Economic Development in Egypt*, The Rand Corporation, 1969.
——: Employment and Wages in Rural Egypt, *American Economic Review*, June 1969.
Hansen, B. and G. Marzouk: *Development and Economic Policy in the U.A.R.*, North-Holland, Amsterdam, 1965.
Hasan, M. S.: *Studies in the Iraqi Economy*, Dar Al-Taliaa, Beirut, 1966. (Arabic)
Harris, G.: *Jordan, its People, its Society, its Culture*, Grove Press, N.Y., 1958.
Henderson, G.: *The Emigration of Highly-Skilled Manpower From the Developing Countries*, United Nations Institute for Training & Research (UNITAR) (mimeo.), N.Y., 1970.
Higgins, B.: *Economic Development*, Norton, N.Y., 1959.
Hilan, Rizkallah: *Culture et Developpement en Syrie et dans les Pays Retardés*, Éditions Anthropos, Paris, 1969.
Himadeh, R.: *The Fiscal System of Lebanon*, Khayat, Beirut, 1961.
Hirschman, A.: Obstacles to Development, *Economic Development and Cultural Change*, July 1965.
Holden, D.: *Farewell to Arabia*, Faber & Faber, London, 1966.
Hopwood, E. (ed.): *The Arabian Peninsula*, Allen & Unwin, London, 1972.
Hoselitz, B. (ed.): *The Progress of Underdeveloped Areas*, Chicago, 1952.
Hoselitz, B.: *Sociological Aspects of Economic Growth*, The Free Press of Glencoe, N.Y., 1960.
——: The City, the Factory and Economic Growth, *American Economic Review, Papers and Proceedings*, 1955.
Hudson, J.: The Litani River of Lebanon, An Example of Middle Eastern Water Development, *Middle East Journal*, Winter 1971.
Hurewitz, J.: *Middle East Politics: The Military Dimension*, Praeger, N.Y., 1969.
—— (ed.): *Soviet-American Rivalry in the Middle East*, Praeger, 1969.
IBRD: *The Economic Development of Syria*, Johns Hopkins Press, Baltimore, 1955.
——: *The Economic Development of Jordan*, Oxford University Press, London, 1957.
——: *The Economic Development of Libya*, Oxford University Press, London, 1960.
——: *The Economic Development of Iraq*, Johns Hopkins Press, Baltimore, 1952.
——: *The Economic Development of Kuwait*, Johns Hopkins Press, Baltimore, 1965.
IFRED: *Le Liban Face À Son Développement*, Beirut, 1963.
I.L.O.: *Yearbooks of Labour Statistics*.
International Institute for Strategic Studies: *The Military Balance*.
Ismael, T.: *Governments & Politics of the Contemporary Middle East*, The Dorsey Press, Illinois, 1970.
Issawi, Charles: *Egypt in Revolution*, Oxford University Press, London, 1963.
——: Economic Development and Liberalism in Lebanon, *Middle East Journal*, Summer 1964.

—— (ed.): *Economic History of the Middle East*, London, 1969.
——: Growth & Structural Change in the Middle East, *Middle East Journal*, Summer 1971.
Issawi, Charles and M. Yeganeh, *The Economics of Middle Eastern Oil*, Faber & Faber, London, 1962.
Jalal, Ferhang: *The Role of Government in the Industrialization of Iraq, 1950-65*, Cass, London, 1972.
Kamerschen, D.: Further Analysis of Over-urbanization, *Economic Development and Cultural Change*, Jan. 1969.
Kanovsky, E.: Arab Economic Unity, *Middle East Journal*, Spring 1967.
——: *The Economic Impact of the Six-Day War*, Praeger, 1970.
Kerr, M.: *The Arab Cold War (1958-67)*, Royal Institute of International Affairs, London, 1967.
Keyrouz, K.: *Reflections on the Most Important Socio-Economic Problems of Contemporary Lebanon*, Lebanese University, Beirut, 1970.
Khalaf, N.: Economic Size and Stability of the Lebanese Economy, *Middle East Economic Papers*, 1967.
Kheir El-Dine, H.: Some Aspects of Regional Differences in the U.A.R., *L'Égypte Contemporaine*, Jan. 1971.
Kitamura, H.: Economic Theory and the Economic Integration of Underdeveloped Regions, in Wionczek, M. (ed.), *Latin American Economic Integration*, Praeger, 1966.
Kubbah, A.: *Libya, Its Oil Industry & Economic System*, The Arab Petro-Economic Research Centre, Baghdad, 1964.
Kuznets, S.: Economic Growth and Income Distribution, *American Economic Review*, 1955.
——: Quantitative Aspects of the Economic Growth of Nations: Distribution of Income by Size, *Economic Development and Cultural Change*, Jan. 1963.
——: *Modern Economic Growth*, Yale University Press, 1966.
——: *Economic Growth and Structure*, Heinemann, London, 1966.
Lampard, E.: The History of Cities in the Economically Advanced Areas, *Economic Development and Cultural Change*, Jan. 1965.
Lapidus, I. (ed.): *Middle Eastern Cities*, University of California Press, Berkeley, 1969.
Lewis, A.: *The Theory of Economic Growth*, Allen & Unwin, London, 1955.
——: Education and Economic Development, *Social and Economic Studies*, June 1961.
Lewis, B.: *The Middle East and the West*, Indiana University Press, Bloomington, 1964.
Mabro, R.: Industrial Growth, Agricultural Under-Employment and the Lewis Model. The Egyptian Case, 1937-1965, *The Journal of Development Studies*, July 1967,
Marchal, J. and Ducros, B. (eds.): *The Distribution of National Income*, Macmillan, N.Y., 1968.
Mayfield, J.: *Rural Politics in Nasser's Egypt*, University of Texas Press, Austin, 1971.
Mcloughlin, F.: The Sudan's Three Towns: A Demographic and Economic Profile of an African Urban Complex, *Economic Development and Cultural Change*, Oct. 1963, Jan. 1964 and April 1964.
Mead, D.: *Growth and Structural Change in the Egyptian Economy*, The Economic Growth Center, Yale University, Illinois, 1967.
Meyer, A. J.: *Middle Eastern Capitalism*, Cambridge, Harvard Press, 1959.
Mikesell, R.: The Theory of Common Markets and Developing Countries, in Robson, P. (ed.): *International Economic Integration*, Penguin, 1971.
Mishan, E.: *The Costs of Economic Growth*, Staples Press, London, 1967.
Mohie-El-Din, A.: *Agricultural Investment and Employment in Egypt Since 1935*, Unpublished Ph.D. thesis, London University, 1966.
Morgan, T.: Distribution of Income in Developed and Under-Developed Countries, *Economic Journal*, 1956.

Musrey, A.: *An Arab Common Market, A Study in Inter-Arab Trade Relations, 1920-67*, Praeger, N.Y., 1969.
Myrdal, G.: *The Challenge of World Poverty*, Pelican, London, 1971.
——: *Asian Drama*, Pelican, London, 1968.
National Bank of Egypt: *Economic Bulletin.*
Nolte, R. (ed.): *The Modern Middle East*, Prentice-Hall International, London, 1963.
O'Brien, P.: *The Revolution in Egypt's Economic System*, Oxford University Press, 1966.
O.E.C.D.: *Development Assistance.*
Osman, A. A.: *Planning, Agricultural Policies and Policy Implementation in the Republic of the Sudan*, Unpublished Ph.D. thesis, Michigan State University, 1968.
Patai, R.: The Dynamics of Westernization in the Middle East, *Middle East Journal*, Winter 1955.
Pearson, L.: *Partners in Development*, Praeger, 1969.
Polk, W. (ed.): *Developmental Revolution: North Africa, Middle East, South Asia*, The Middle East Institute, Washington, 1963.
Qubain, F.: *Education and Science in the Arab World*, Johns Hopkins Press, Baltimore, 1966.
Ragheb, I.: Patterns of Urban Growth in the Middle East, in Breese, G. (ed.): *The City in the Newly Developing Countries*, Princeton University, 1969.
Republic of Iraq: *Statistical Handbook*, 1957-67, Baghdad, 1968.
Republic of Lebanon, Ministry of Agriculture, Rural Economic Institute: *Agriculture in the Lebanese Economy* (mimeo.), 1968.
Riad, H.: *L'Égypte Nasserienne*, Les Éditions de Minuit, Paris, 1964.
Rivlin, B. and J. Szyliowicz (eds.): *The Contemporary Middle East, Tradition and Innovation*, Random House, N.Y., 1965.
Rostow, W.: *The Stages of Economic Growth*, Cambridge University Press, 1962.
——: *Politics and the Stages of Growth*, Cambridge University Press, Cambridge, 1971.
Saab, C.: *The Egyptian Agrarian Reform, 1952-62*, Oxford University Press, 1967.
Saudi Arabia, Ministry of Finance and National Economy: *Statistical Yearbook*, 1969.
Saudi Arabia: *Annual Reports.*
Saudi Arabian Monetary Agency: *Statistical Summary.*
Sayegh, K.: *Oil and Arab Regional Development*, Praeger, 1968.
Sayigh, Y.: *Entrepreneurs of Lebanon*, Harvard University Press, Cambridge, Massachusetts, 1962.
Sayigh, Y. and M. Atallah: *A Second Look at the Lebanese Economy*, Dar Al-Taliaa, Beirut, 1966. (Arabic)
Sharayha, W.: *Economic Development in Jordan*, Institute of Arab Studies, Cairo, 1970. (Arabic)
Stickley, S. and Others (eds.): *Man, Food & Agriculture in the Middle East*, American University of Beirut, Beirut, 1969.
Suleiman, M.: *Political Parties in Lebanon*, Cornell University Press, N.Y., 1967.
Tansky, L.: *U.S. and U.S.S.R. Aid to Developing Countries*, Praeger, 1967.
Thompson, J. and R. Reischauer (eds.): *Modernization of the Arab World*, Nostrand, Princeton, 1966.
Toynbee, A.: *Cities on the Move*, Oxford University Press, 1970.
U.A.R., Central Agency for Public Mobilization and Statistics: *Population Growth in the U.A.R. and its Challenges to Development*, Cairo, 1966. (Arabic)
——: *Statistical Indicators*, Cairo, 1966.
U.A.R., Ministry of Planning: *Follow-Up and Evaluation Report of the First Five-Year Plan*, (mimeo.), Feb. 1966.
——: *Follow-Up and Evaluation of Economic Development in the U.A.R.*, 1965/6-68/9.

Ul-Haq, Mahbub: Employment, Income Distribution in 1970's: A New Perspective, *Development Digest*, Oct. 1971.

U.N., Department of Economic Affairs: *Review of Economic Conditions in the Middle East*, 1950, 1951.

U.N.: *Economic Development in the Middle East, 1945-54*, N.Y., 1955.

——: *The External Financing of Economic Development: International Flow of Long-Term Capital and Official Donations*, N.Y., 1968, 1969 and 1970.

——: *Report on the World Social Situation*, 1963 & 1970.

——: *Structure and Growth of Selected African Economics* (mimeo.), 1958.

——: *Survey of Economic Conditions in Africa*, 1968, N.Y., 1972.

U.N., Technical Assistance Programme: *The Economic and Social Development of Libya*, N.Y., 1953.

——: *Urbanization: Development Policies and Planning*, International Development Review, No. 1, N.Y., 1968.

——: *Statistical Yearbooks.*

——: *Demographic Yearbooks.*

——: *Yearbooks of National Accounts Statistics.*

——: *Yearbooks of International Trade Statistics.*

UNESCO: *Statistical Yearbook.*

——: *The Organization and Financing of Literacy Campaigns in Arab Countries*, Serse El-Layyan, Egypt, 1965. (Arabic)

UNESOB: *La Croissance Économique et Le Niveau de Qualification de la Population Active dans Divers Pays au Moyen-Orient* (mimeo.), April 1971.

——: *Environmental Implications of Urban Settlements; Issues of Urban Ecology in the Middle East*, (mimeo.), Sept. 1971.

——: *Étude Comparative des Cadres Institutionnels du Commerce Intra-Marché CommunArab*, (mimeo.), June 1971.

——: *Long-Term Prospects in the Development of Selected Countries and Sub-Regions of the Middle East*, (mimeo.), 1971.

——: *Report of the Symposium on Industrial Development In Arab Countries*, N.Y., 1967.

——: *Studies on Selected Development Problems in Various Countries in the Middle East*, 1967-70.

Van der Meulen, D.: *The Wells of Ibn Saud*, J. Murray, London, 1957.

Vatikiotis, P.: *The Modern History of Egypt*, Weidenfeld & Nicholson, London, 1969.

——: *Conflict in the Middle East*, Allen & Unwin, London, 1971.

—— (ed.): *Egypt Since the Revolution*, Allen & Unwin, London, 1968.

——: *Revolution in the Middle East and Other Case Studies*, Allen & Unwin, London, 1972.

Wahba, J.: *Surplus Labour and the Choice of Techniques In Egypt*, Unpublished M.Sc., thesis, The American University in Cairo, 1971.

Warriner, D.: *Land Reform and Economic Development in the Middle East*, Oxford, 1962.

——: Land Reform, Employment and Income in the Middle East, *International Labour Review*, June 1970.

Waterson, A.: On Planning Economic Development, *Economic Development and Cultural Change*, July 1965.

——: *Development Planning, Lessons of Experience*, Johns Hopkins Press, Baltimore, 1969.

Wazzan, S.: *From Backwardness to Socialist Development in the Agricultural Sector*, Damascus, 1967. (Arabic)

Wickwar, W.: *Modernization of Administration in the Middle East*, Beirut, Khayat, 1963.

Wionczok, M. (ed.): *Economic Cooperation in Latin America, Africa and Asia*, M I T Press, Cambridge, Massachusetts, 1969.

Wynn, R.: The Sudan's 10-Year Plan of Economic Development, 1961/2-70/1: An Analysis of Achievement to 1967/8, *The Journal of Developing Areas*, July 1971.

INDEX